James G Miall

Suggestions in brickwork with illustrations from the architecture of Italy

Together with a catalogue of bricks made by the Hydraulic-Press Brick Companies

James G Miall

Suggestions in brickwork with illustrations from the architecture of Italy
Together with a catalogue of bricks made by the Hydraulic-Press Brick Companies

ISBN/EAN: 9783742888662

Manufactured in Europe, USA, Canada, Australia, Japa

Cover: Foto ©Andreas Hilbeck / pixelio.de

Manufactured and distributed by brebook publishing software (www.brebook.com)

James G Miall

Suggestions in brickwork with illustrations from the architecture of Italy

SUGGESTIONS IN BRICKWORK

WITH

ILLUSTRATIONS FROM THE ARCHI-
TECTURE OF ITALY, TOGETHER
WITH A CATALOGUE OF
BRICKS MADE BY THE
HYDRAULIC-PRESS
BRICK COM-
PANIES

WASHINGTON HYDRAULIC-PRESS BRICK
COMPY, WASHINGTON, D.C., MDCCCXCV

Copyright, 1895
by
The Eastern Hydraulic-Press Brick Company

All rights reserved

PRICE, THREE DOLLARS

Printed by J. B. Lippincott Company, Philadelphia, U. S. A.

CONTENTS

PART FIRST

SUGGESTIONS IN DESIGN

ARCADES AND LOGGIE. PAGE
    An Arcade 7
    A Loggia or Window . 9
    A Nave Arcade . . 11

DOORWAYS AND ENTRANCES.
    An Entrance . . 13
    A Doorway . . . 15
    An Arched Entrance . 17

WINDOWS.

	PAGE
A Group of Windows .	19
A Renaissance Window	21
An Arched Window	23

MOULDED BANDS.

Architraves .	25
Arch Mouldings .	27

CORNICES.

Two Cornices	29
Two Cornices	31
Two Cornices	33

BRICK MOSAICS.

Bands and Diapers	35
Friezes and Bands	37
Floor Mosaics and Borders	39

FIRE-PLACES.

A Chimney-Piece for a Large Room .	41
A Chimney-Piece for an Entrance Hall .	43
Two Fire-Places .	45
A Chimney-Piece .	47

BALCONIES.

A Balcony	49
A Balcony and Loggia	49

PIERS AND COLUMNS.

A Pier and Arch	51
A Pier and Arch	53
A Group of Columns	55
Circular Piers	57

GATE POSTS.

Gate Posts and Wall Piers	59

PART SECOND

CATALOGUE OF SHAPES

		PAGE
	INDEX TO BRICK NUMBERS	63
A	STANDARD AND ROMAN BRICKS	67
B	ANGLE BRICKS, JAMB AND ARCH MOULDINGS	71
C	RADIUS BRICKS	85
D	JAMB AND ARCH MOULDINGS	89
E	PANEL MOULDINGS	111
F	STRING COURSES	117
G	CORNICE MOULDINGS	143
H	BASE MOULDINGS	151
K	ORNAMENTAL BRICKS	157

PART THIRD

INSTRUCTIONS FOR ORDERING

	PAGE
GENERAL	183
SEMI-CIRCULAR ARCHES	184
SEGMENT ARCHES	185
ELLIPTIC ARCHES	186
GOTHIC ARCHES	187
FLAT ARCHES	188
SEGMENT ARCHES WITH FLAT TOPS	190
MITRES	191

PART FOURTH

CONCLUSION

	PAGE
THE HYDRAULIC-PRESS	194
THE COMPANIES	195

ILLUSTRATIONS

	PAGE
CREMONA. THE TOWER OF THE CATHEDRAL .	i
SIENA. THE PALAZZO PUBBLICO, FROM THE BACK. *Frontispiece*.	ii
SAN GIUSTINO. THE CASTLE	v
MURANO. THE APSE OF SAN DONATO	ix
CARPI. THE CATHEDRAL.	xi
TAORMINA. A WINDOW .	2
PIACENZA. PART OF THE PALAZZO COMMUNALE	4
BOLOGNA. PALAZZO MALVASIA	60

		PAGE
PIACENZA.	PALAZZO COMMUNALE	63
HERCULANEUM.	ROMAN BRICKWORK	67
BOLOGNA.	CASA VECCHIETTI	71
ROME.	SS. GIOVANNI E PAOLO SUL CELIO	85
PIACENZA.	PALAZZO COMMUNALE. DETAIL	89
ASSISI.	THE SMALLER CLOISTER OF S. FRANCESCO	111
ORVIETO.	WINDOWS FROM THE PALAZZO DEL CAPITANO	117
ROME.	SAN GIORGIO IN VELABRO	143
POMPEII.	COLUMNS FROM THE BASILICA	151
BOLOGNA.	ARCHES FROM THE PALAZZO FAVA	157
SIENA.	A NARROW STREET	180
BOLOGNA.	CASA DEI CARACCI	182
MODENA.	THE NAVE OF THE CATHEDRAL	192

The Emperors' heads used as ornaments in this volume are reproduced from wood engravings by Heinrich Vogtherr, in Crispiani's " Kaiserchronik," Strasbourg, 1541.

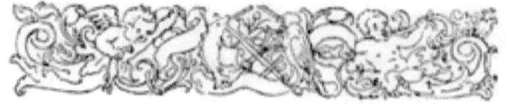

INTRODUCTION

OF late there has been a notable improvement in brickwork in the United States, yet the use of moulded and enriched bricks is by no means so general as the variety of shapes obtainable warrants. This has been largely due to the difficulty of finding forms suitable for a given place. This book has been prepared to overcome the difficulty so far as it affects the product of "Hydraulic-press" brick companies, and to afford suggestions as to their use in architectural compositions. It is hoped that the separation of the several kinds of bricks into groups (e. g., jambs, arches, bases, cornices, etc.) attempted in Part Second, will facilitate the selection of those desired from among the large number of profiles there shown. The thanks of the companies are due to Mr. Frank Miles Day, under whose direction this book has been prepared, and from whose collection the illustrations have been selected.

AN ARCADE

ELEVATIONS for arcades are given on the opposite page, and also on pages fifty-one, fifty-three, fifty-five, and fifty-seven. The arch is repeated as many times as necessary, and in various places; for example, as a loggia under the porch as an arcade, carrying part of a building. A single arch of this character may be used for a doorway, as suggested in the sketch in the lower part of the illustration. Singly, or in a series of two or three, such arches may be used to form an important window. These arches can be furnished of any desired radius. Those shown in the drawing are three feet in radius. If a greater degree of enrichment be desired in the arch mouldings, the egg and dart, No. 506, or the water-leaf, No. 304, or both, may be substituted for the plain mouldings shown in the drawing. The column shown in this illustration is octagonal, and about twelve and a half inches in diameter. The capitals may be of stone or terra-cotta, carved or moulded. The bases would naturally be of the same material as the caps.

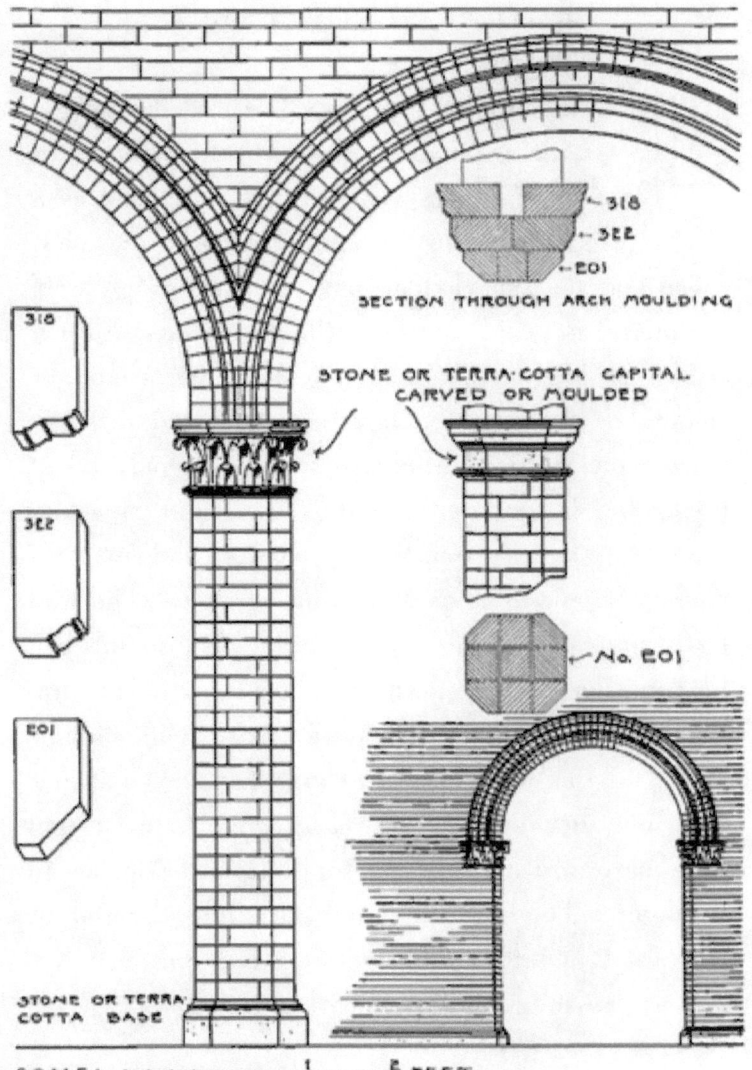

A LOGGIA OR WINDOW

THE illustration suggests an arched window, either triple, as shown in the sketch, or double or single, as desired. If used as a window, the boxes are concealed behind the pier, which may be semi-circular, as shown in the left arch, or square, as in the central arch. If used as an open arcade or loggia, the piers may be either round or square, or stone shafts may be substituted. If the square pier is used, the caps and bases may be of brick; but if the round shaft is used, the caps and bases will be of stone or terra-cotta, and may, of course, be enriched, as shown on the left. The wall bases may, in any case, be of brick. The arches can be furnished of any desired radius. In the illustration their radius is one foot ten inches. The columns shown in this illustration are four feet seven inches in height, including cap and base, and, whether round or square, are about eight and a quarter inches in diameter. The sill will be of stone or terra-cotta, or, if desired, of bricks on edge, for which purpose No. 505 will be suitable.

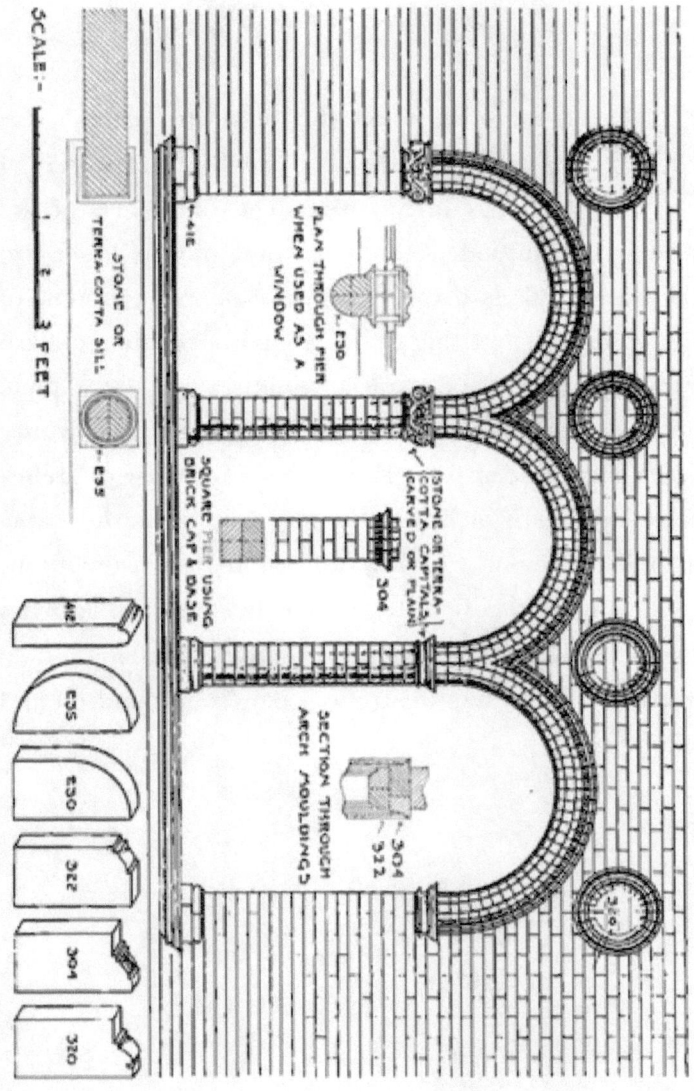

A NAVE ARCADE

THE suggestion on the opposite page is for the nave arcade of a church, the interior of which is brickwork. The only parts of the design not intended to be carried out in brick are the caps and bases of the nave piers, columns of the triforium, and the pierced slab above them; these would preferably be made of stone. The nave piers are about two feet eight inches in diameter and twenty feet centre to centre. The radius of the large arches is ten feet six inches. Slightly modified, the same sketch will answer as a motif for an extensive front. One bay of the first floor may be modified into an important entrance. The effect of a similar arcade may be seen in the illustration, page one hundred and ninety-two.

II

AN ENTRANCE TO AN IMPORTANT BUILDING

IN this example of the use of plain and moulded bricks, the entire composition is of brickwork, except the columns, the pilaster-caps and bases, and the circular slabs, which are marble, and the keystone and consoles, which are terra-cotta. The pavement of the vestibule is a mosaic of colored brickwork. For additional brick mosaics, see pages thirty-five, thirty-seven, and thirty-nine. The opening is twenty feet six inches high, and nine feet wide from column to column. Should the building be of sufficient size, the same motif could be used for a loggia; as such it may be seen in perspective on page forty-nine.

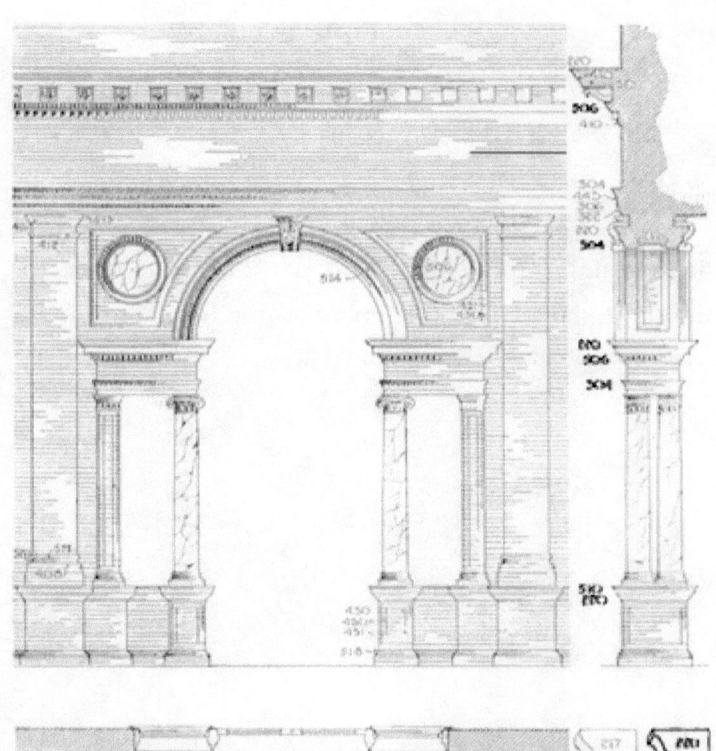

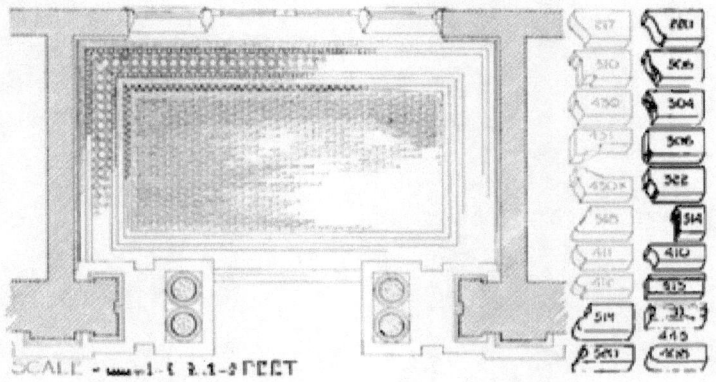

SCALE - 1 : 2, 1 = 2 FEET

A DOORWAY

A SUGGESTION is here offered as to the use of bricks in forming a simple, classical, or Renaissance doorway. The head is carried on a suitable iron bar. The size of the opening of the door shown in the sketch is three feet nine inches wide by seven feet high.

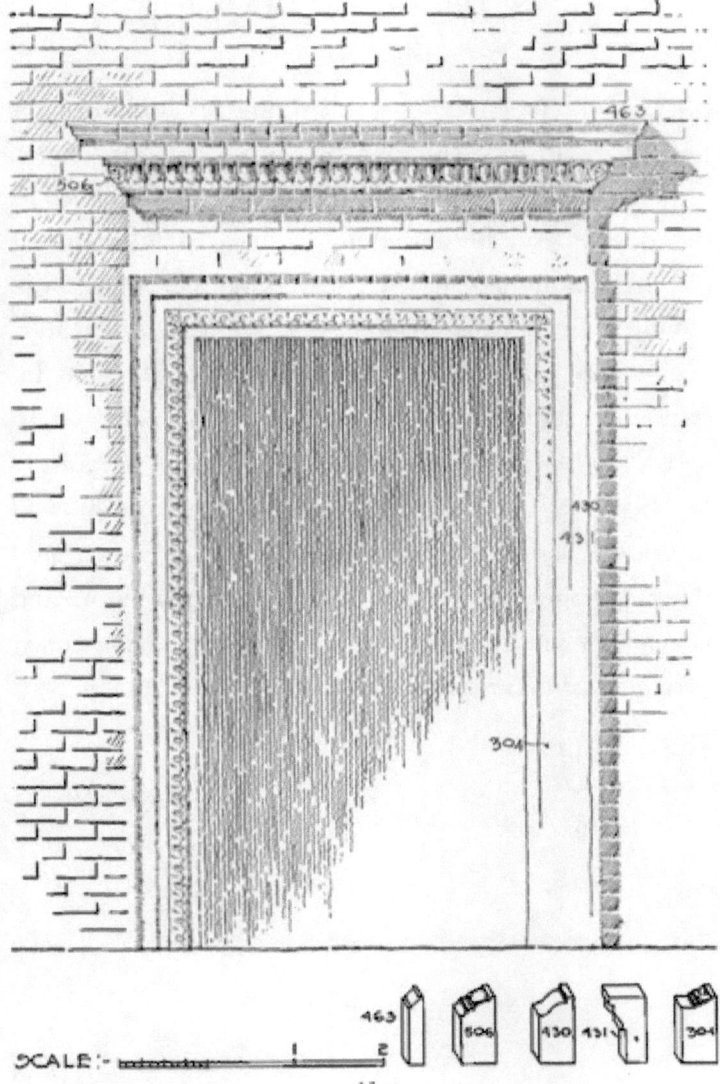

AN ARCHED ENTRANCE

THIS example shows a simple treatment of an entrance suitable for a bank, a dwelling, or a small semi-public building. The effect of this design may be varied by increasing the width of the arch moulding and a greater degree of richness obtained by the use of the egg and dart and waterleaf. The soffit of the arch may be made plain instead of panelled. The reveal may be changed to suit a wall of any thickness. The design is entirely for brickwork, except that the steps are stone and the doors of wood. The arch is five feet radius, and the door-opening eleven feet six inches high, and seven feet nine inches wide. These dimensions may, of course, be varied at will.

311
513
220
431
408
410
411
412
SCALE
FEET

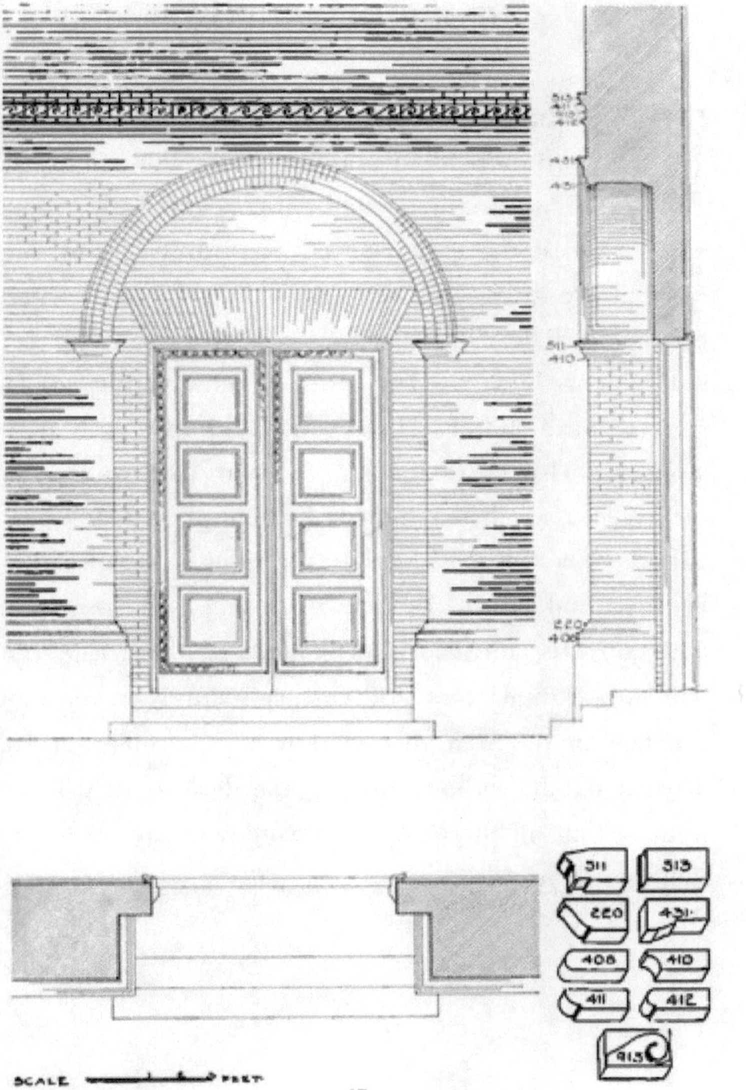

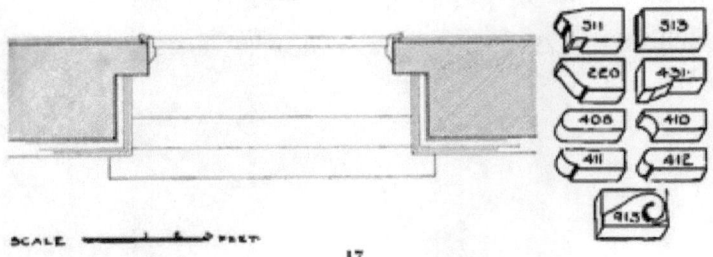

A GROUP OF WINDOWS

THE upper window, which is Italian gothic in style, is all of brick except the columns. This window might be used with good effect, even if the columns, the small arches, and the work above them, enclosed within the large arch, were removed. The clear opening in that case would be nine feet six inches. The lower window to the left is suitable for a church. Brickwork alternates with arch stones. The clear opening is four feet wide and eleven feet six inches high. This may, of course, be varied. The lower window to the right is Renaissance in style, and is all of brickwork except its stone sill and the three terra-cotta ornaments of the arch. By widening the pilasters, and correspondingly increasing the face of the arch, this window may be enlarged to a great extent without injuring the design. It will be noticed that all three of these windows may be modified into doorways.

A RENAISSANCE WINDOW

 SUGGESTION is here offered for the use of brick in a window of Renaissance form. The transom and head are carried on suitable iron bars. In this sketch the lower openings are each three feet wide, and five feet six inches high, while the upper are three feet square. By varying these dimensions, this window may be made to harmonize with surrounding proportions, other than those for which it was specially designed.

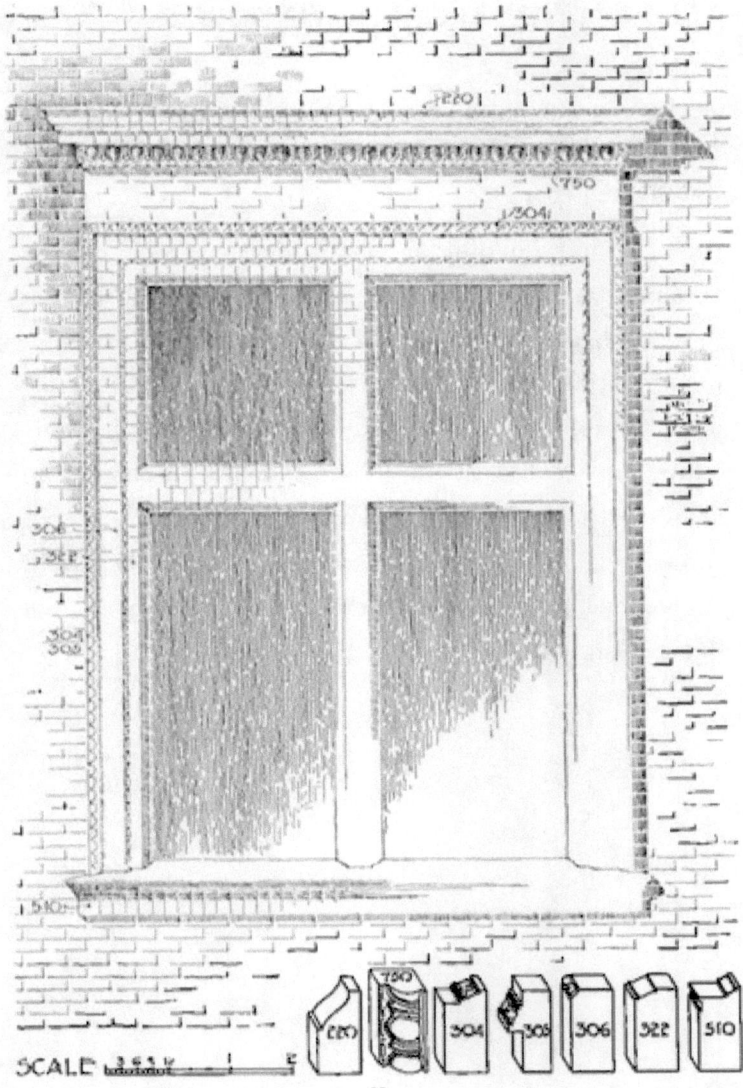

AN ARCHED WINDOW

THIS example is entirely of brickwork, excepting the sill and the column. Even these may be made of brick by using No. 505 for the sill, and building a small pier in place of the column. It should be noted that the bricks of the outer arch are not ground, but that the circular arrangement is produced by using a wedge-shaped mortar-joint, the effect of which is very good where the radius is not too small. In the illustration the radius of the smaller arches is thirteen inches, and of the larger three feet. These may, of course, be varied at will. A somewhat similar window may be seen in the illustration, page two.

463
463
412
499
412
463
SCALE:- 1 2 3 4 FEET

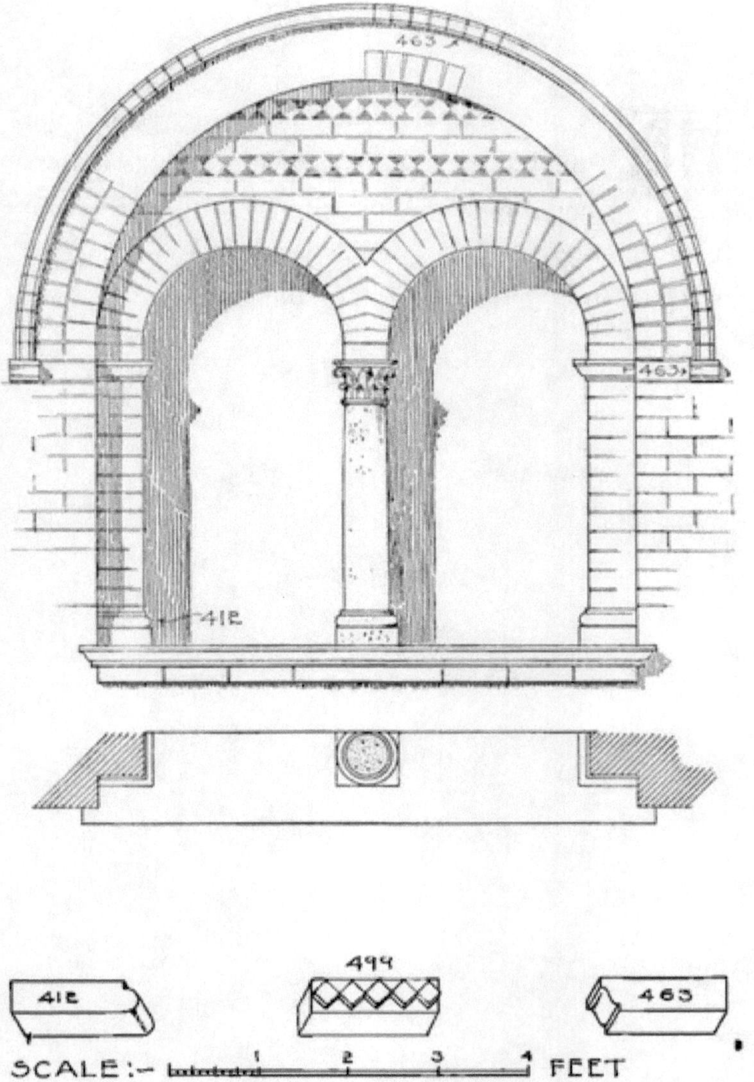

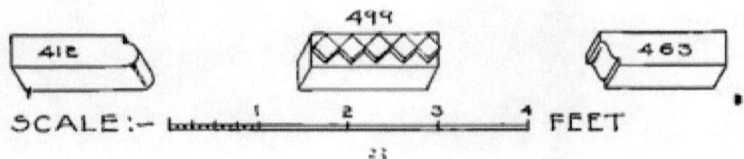

ARCHITRAVES

THE sketches opposite afford suggestions for the treatment of architraves around windows and doors. Those shown are enriched in various ways. Plain moulded architraves may be selected from parts B and D of the catalogue.

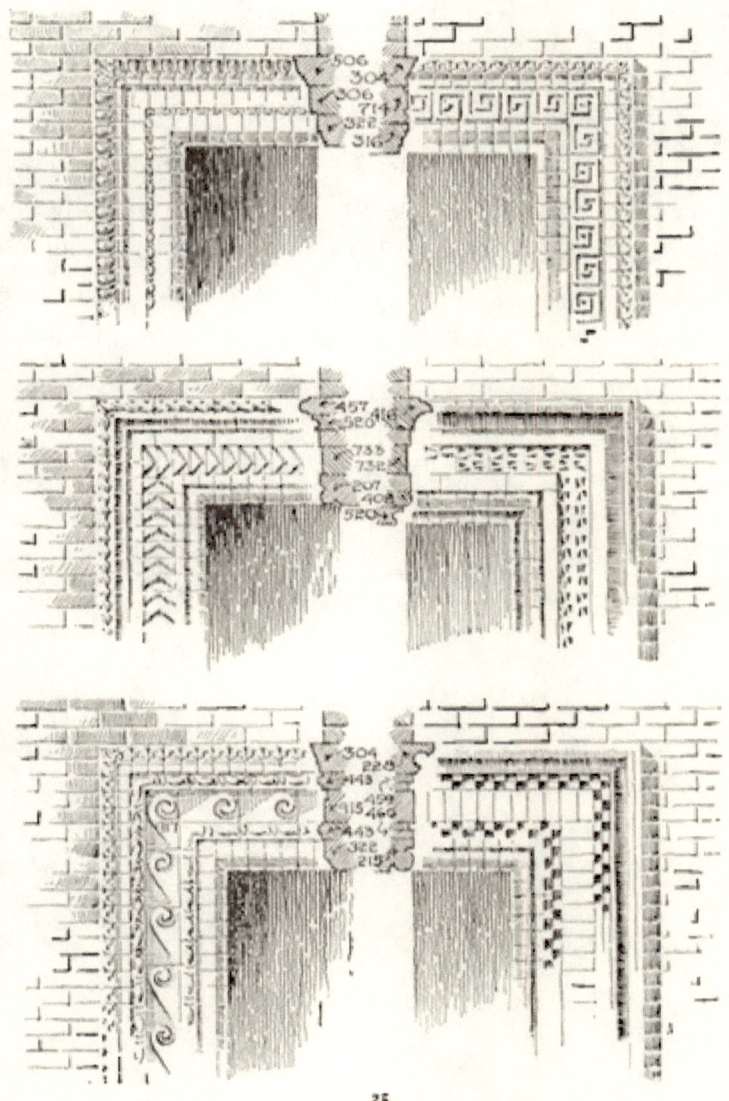

ARCH MOULDINGS

THE designs on the opposite page afford suggestions for the treatment of arch mouldings. Some of them are plain and others enriched, and they are of various widths, from four inches to sixteen inches. Other bricks suitable for similar purposes will be found in parts B and D of the catalogue, as well as among the ornamental bricks, part K.

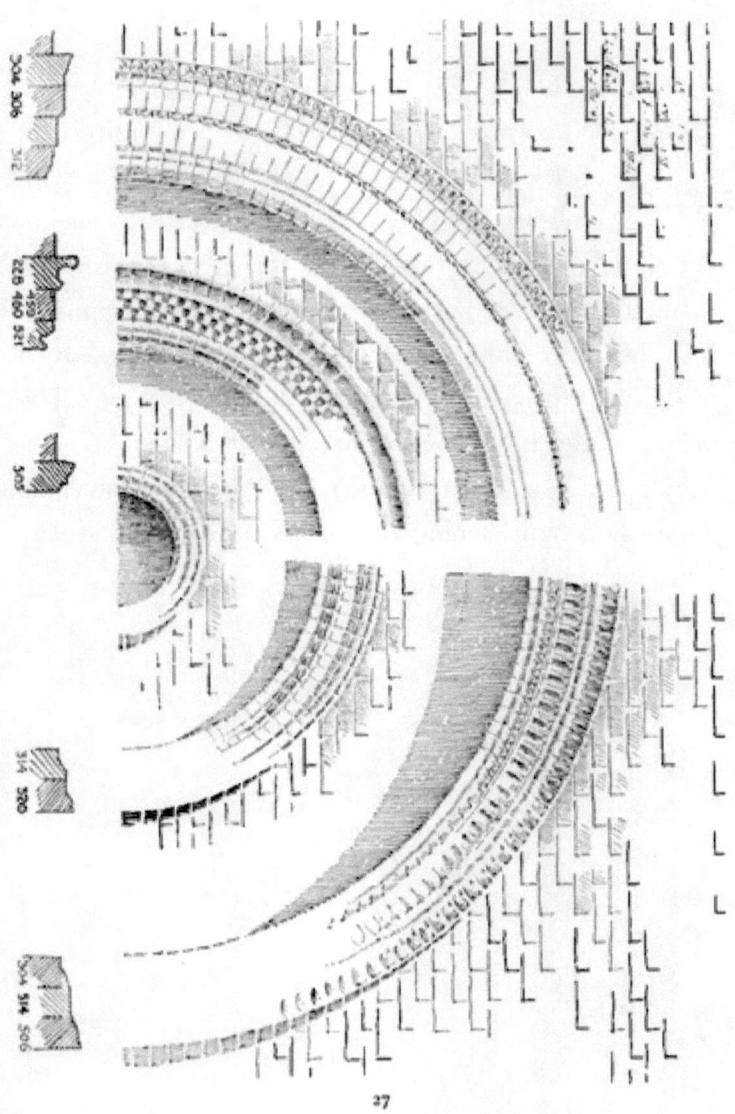

CORNICES

THE cornices shown opposite are entirely of brickwork. The upper is provided with overhanging eaves, the rafter-ends being cut to a pattern. In the lower no eaves are shown. In either case they may be used or not, as required. The height of the upper cornice is about sixteen inches; its projection is about thirteen inches. The height of the lower cornice is about two feet; its projection is about fourteen inches. Projections may be diminished by lessening the overhang of the corona.

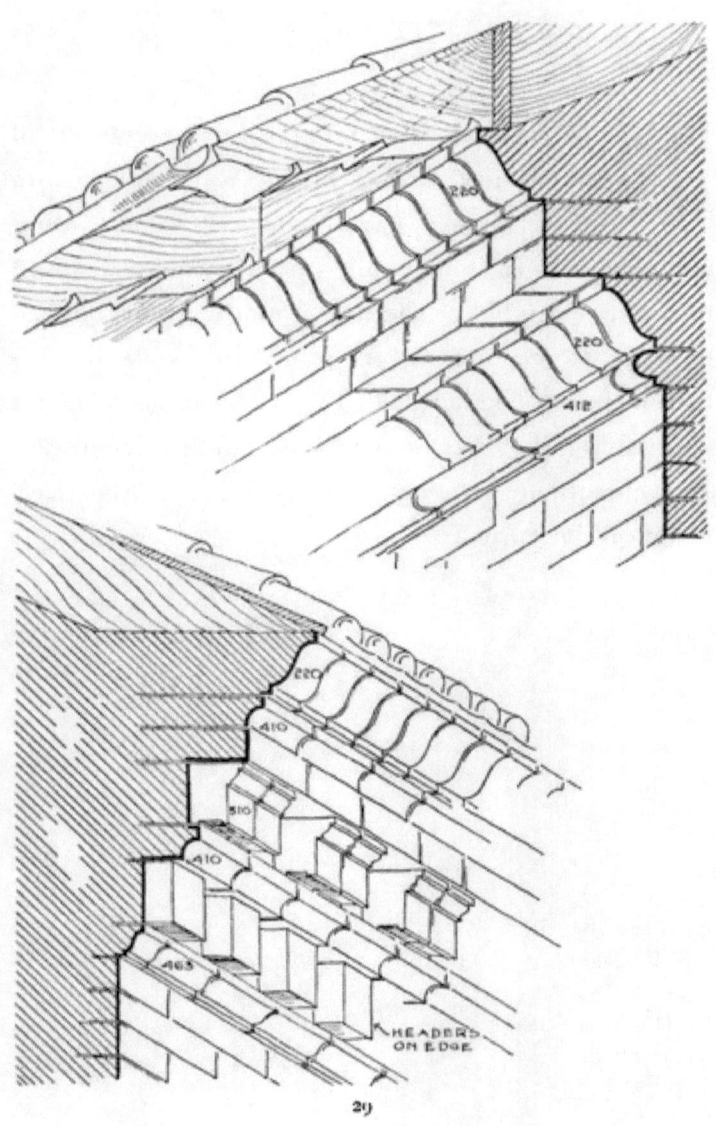

29

CORNICES

THE cornices shown opposite are entirely of brickwork. The upper is provided with overhanging eaves, the rafter-ends being cut to a pattern. In either case they may be used or not, as required. The height of the upper cornice is about twenty inches; its projection is about fourteen inches. The height of the lower cornice is about seventeen inches; its projection is about twelve inches. Projections may be diminished by lessening the overhang of the corona.

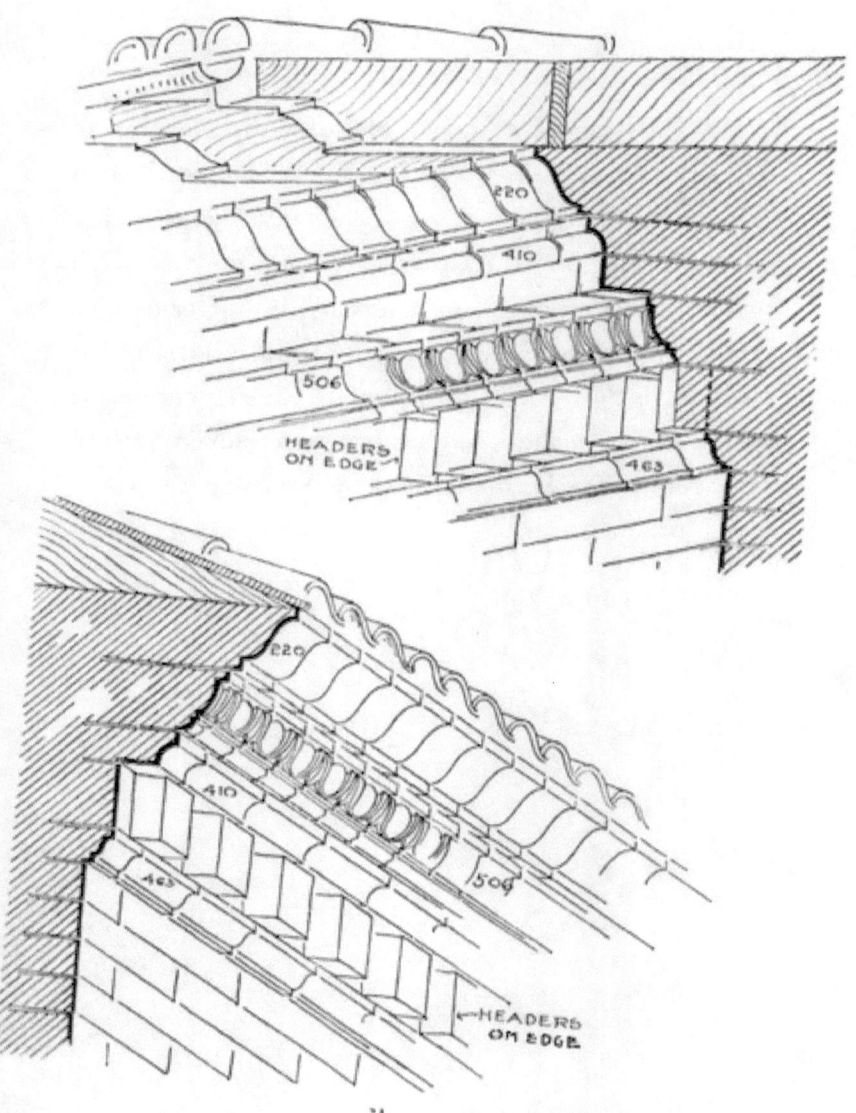

CORNICES

THE cornices shown opposite are entirely of brickwork. The upper is provided with overhanging eaves, the rafter-ends being cut to a pattern. In either case they may be used or not, as required. The height of the upper cornice is about three feet six inches; its projection is about fourteen inches. The height of the lower cornice is about twelve inches; its projection is seven inches. Projections may be diminished by lessening the overhang of the corona.

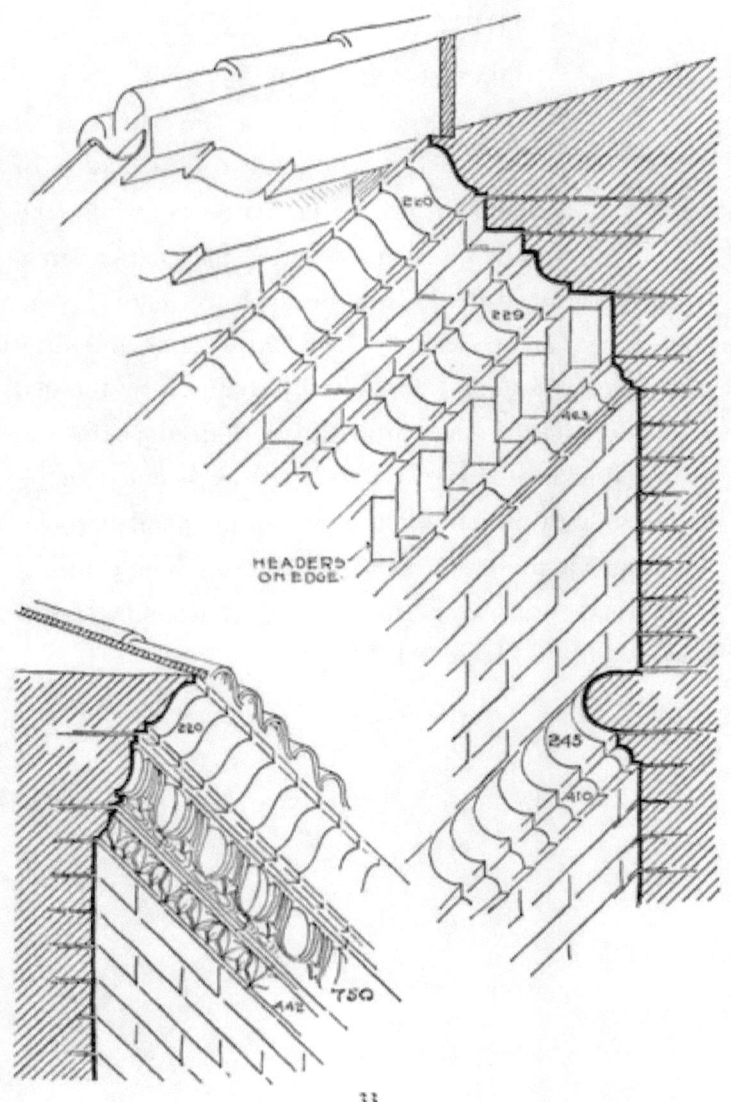

HEADERS ON EDGE

BRICK MOSAICS
BANDS AND DIAPERS

THE upper diagrams suggest possibilities of arrangement in band patterns, while the lower give two patterns for diaper-work. It will be noticed that all the designs are made by the uniform use of stretchers. The proportions and sizes of the designs could be materially changed by the use of headers. The pattern at the bottom suggests the use of bricks of three different shades,—one for the body of the wall, one for the simple diagonal pattern, the other for the more intricate pattern. The coloring is optional; but, as a rule, strong contrasts in such work should be avoided.

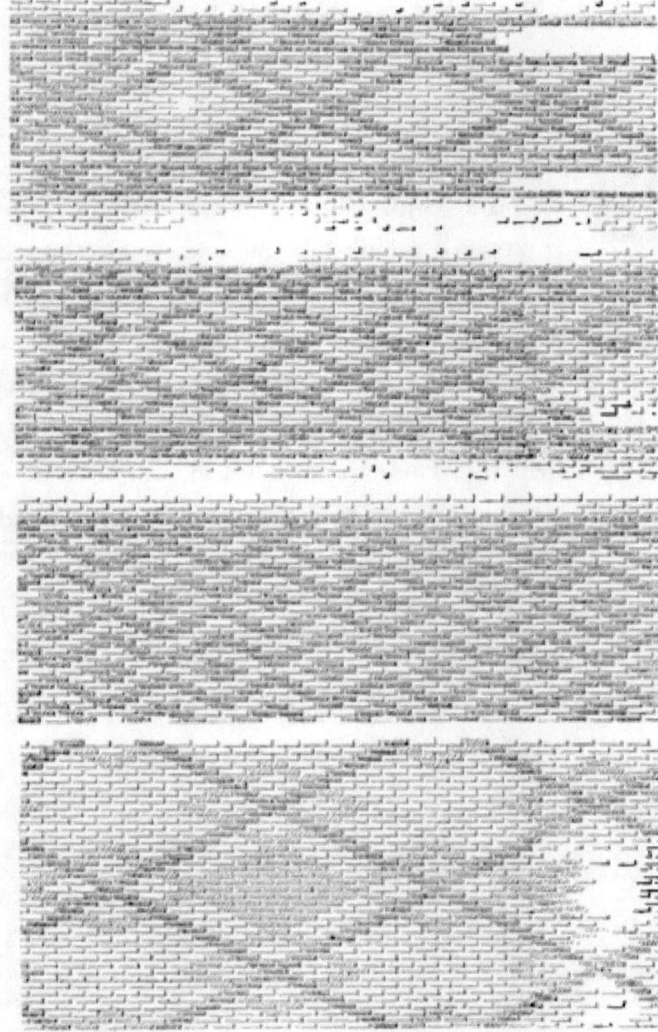

SCALE: 1 2 3 FEET.

BRICK MOSAICS
FRIEZES AND BANDS

THESE diagrams suggest possibilities in friezes or broad wall bands. Much stronger contrasts are admissible in such work than in the all-over pattern shown on page thirty-five. The expense of grinding bricks to such small pieces, as shown in some of the secondary bands, may be obviated by the use of whole bricks of solid color, producing nearly the same general effect, but less crisp in detail. Attention is called to the ease with which the Greek fret can be made: a simple halving being the only cut necessary. The bands are drawn seven feet four inches in width, but this may be varied at will.

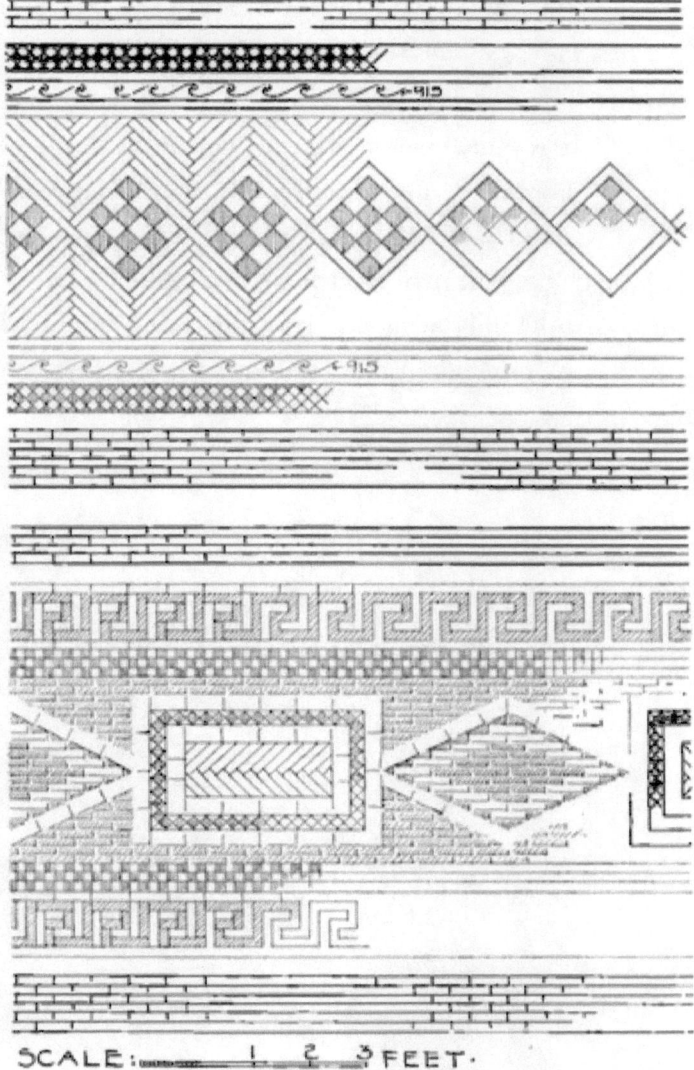

SCALE: 1 2 3 FEET.

BRICK MOSAICS
FLOORS AND BORDERS

BRICK pavements with ornamented borders might be more frequently employed with good effect than at present. The opposite diagrams suggest two treatments suitable for vestibules. Another is seen on page thirteen. The first design is of bricks laid flat; the second, of bricks on edge.

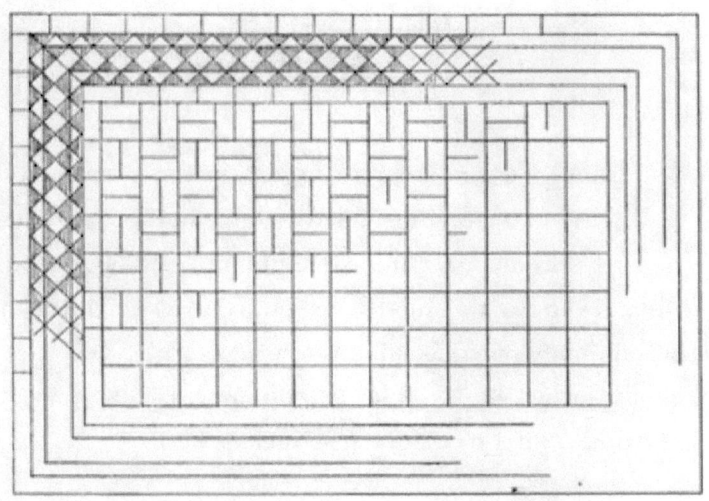

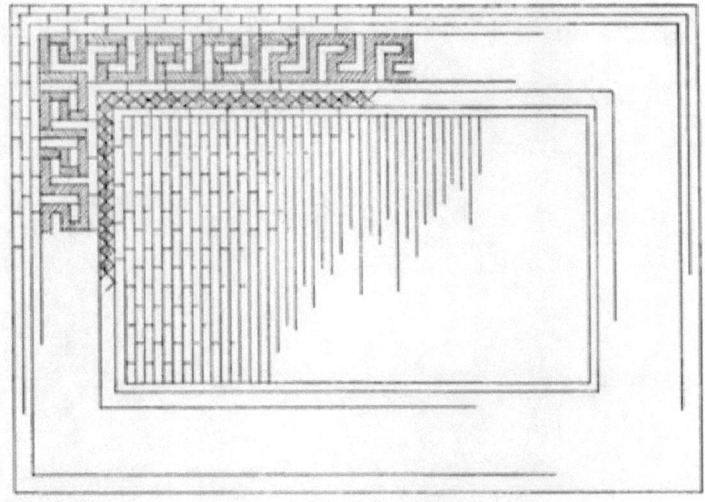

SCALE. 1 2 3 FEET.

A CHIMNEY-PIECE
FOR A LARGE ROOM

OPPOSITE is seen a suggestion for a chimney-piece, suitable for a club, hotel, railroad station, or other semi-public building. The design, even to the hearth, is entirely of brickwork. This chimney-piece is about ten feet wide, and ten feet six inches high. The fire opening is about four feet wide, and three feet five inches high.

A CHIMNEY-PIECE FOR
AN ENTRANCE HALL

THE design suggests a chimney-piece suitable for a hall-way or other large room. It is entirely of brickwork, except the keystone, and is about nine feet six inches wide, and seven feet three inches high. The fire-place radius is two feet. This design shows the manner in which moulded bricks adapt themselves to use in forming arches of small radius.

TWO FIRE-PLACES

THE upper design suggests a simple treatment suitable for dwelling houses. The shelf is, of course, of wood or stone. All other parts, including the hearths, are brickwork. This mantel is about seven feet six inches wide, and five feet high. The fire-opening is three feet six inches wide, and two feet three inches high. The lower fire-place, like the upper, is intended for use in a dwelling. Its greater dimensions and more elaborate design render it suitable for a room of more importance. It is entirely of brick, with the exception of the shelf, which may be of stone or wood. The panels above the shelf may be made more ornate by the use of the water-leaf, No. 304. The chimney-piece is about eight feet six inches wide, and seven feet six inches high. The fire-place opening is four feet wide, and two feet seven inches high.

A CHIMNEY-PIECE

A TREATMENT is here suggested suitable for general use in rooms of moderate size. The design is entirely of brick, including the mantel-shelf and hearth. Other combinations of bricks, such as those shown on page twenty-five, may be used for the enriched band around the opening. The entire mantel is seven feet six inches wide and five feet high. The fire-place opening is three feet wide and two feet seven inches high.

A BALCONY

ON the opposite page a balcony, composed entirely of brickwork, is shown. Its dimensions are, approximately,—length, sixteen feet; projection, three feet six inches; height from bottom of corbels to top of string course, seven feet six inches; from top of string course to top of balcony rail, three feet six inches. This balcony may, of course, be used with three arches in place of four. The amount of projection and depth of corbels, as well as the length of the balcony, can be varied to suit different cases. The illustration to the right shows this balcony and a loggia in perspective. The loggia may readily be modified into a window.

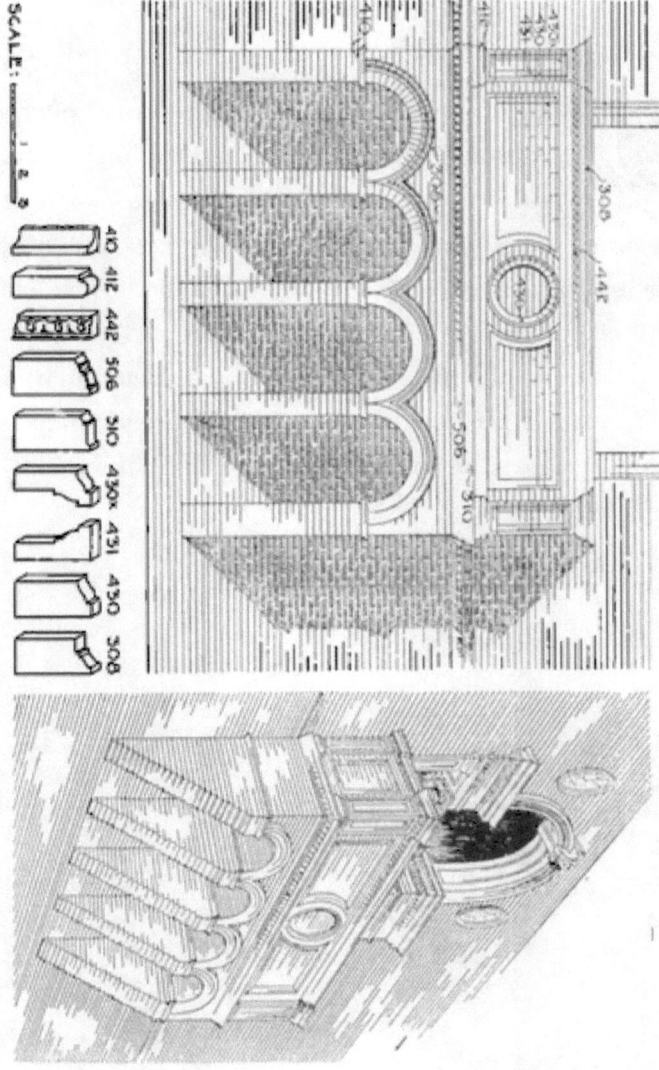

A PIER AND ARCH

ON the opposite page a suggestion is offered for the treatment of a moulded pier, carrying heavy arches. The design is to be executed entirely of brick, except the cap and base, which should properly be made of stone. The pier is about four feet six inches in diameter. With similar combinations of bricks, piers of any diameter may be built. Other treatments of piers and arches may be seen on pages seven, nine, eleven, fifty-three, fifty-five, and fifty-seven.

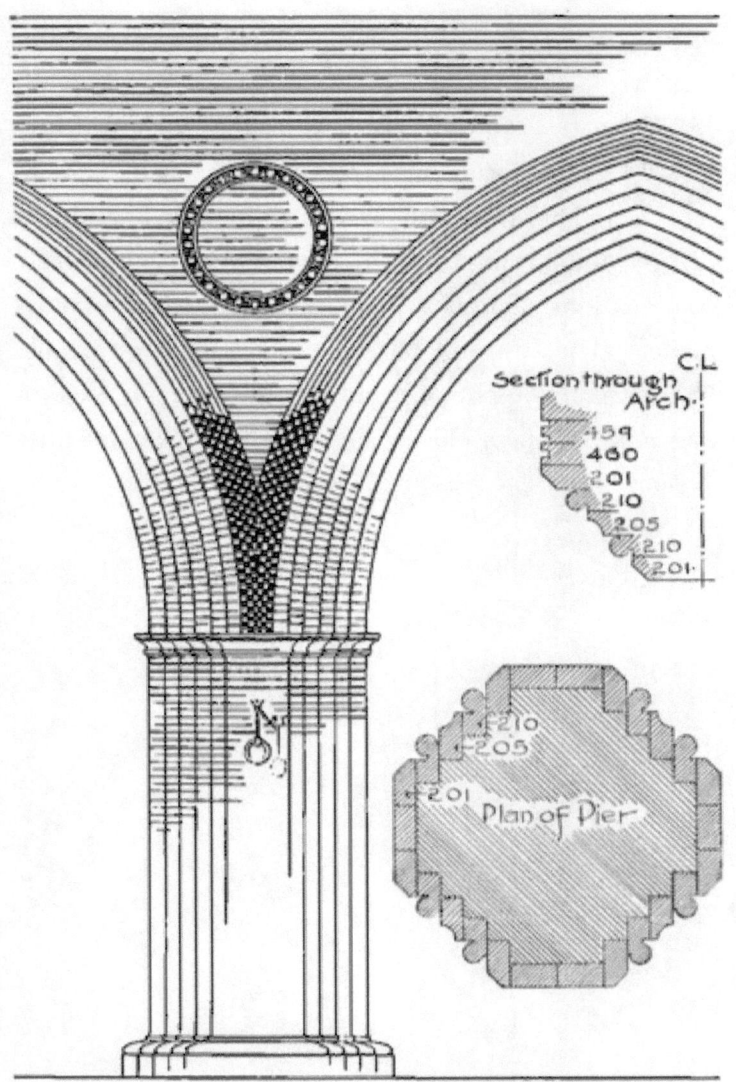

A PIER AND ARCH

ON the opposite page a design is shown suitable for a nave arcade in a small church. The pier and arch are moulded, and the pier is about three feet in diameter. With similar combinations of bricks, piers of various sizes may be made. The cap and base are, of course, of stone. Other treatments of piers and arches may be seen on pages seven, nine, eleven, fifty-one, fifty-five, and fifty-seven.

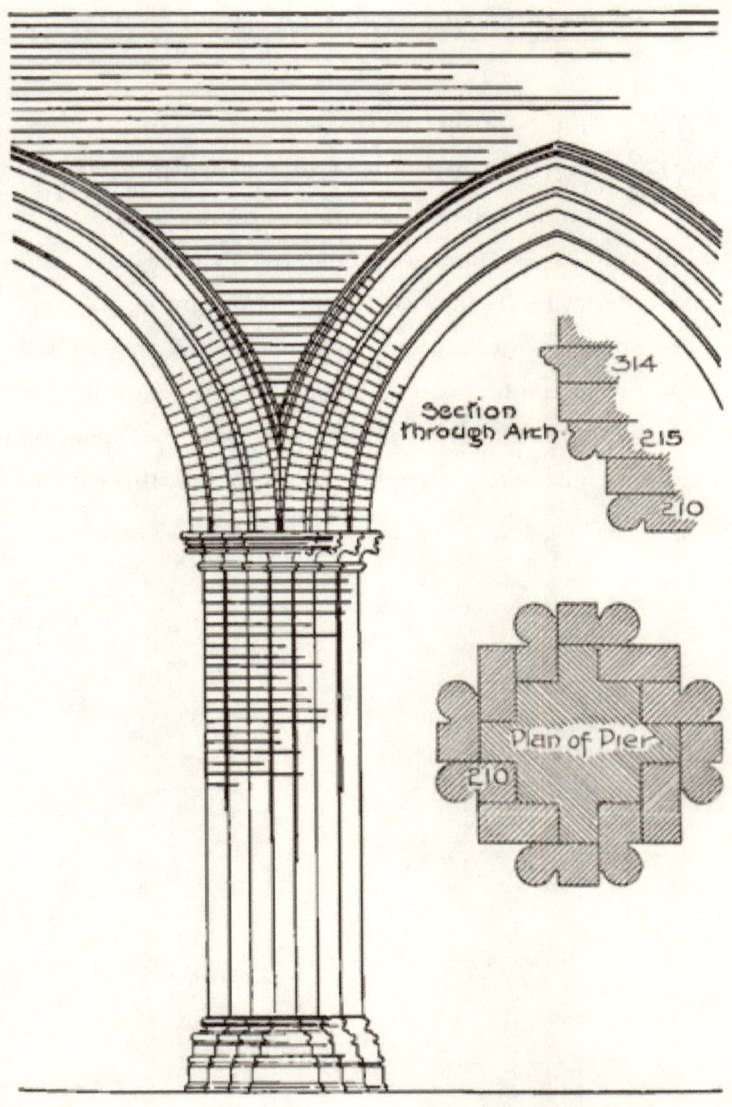

A GROUP OF COLUMNS

IN the opposite design arches are shown springing from a group of either two or four columns, as may seem desirable. These are treated in a Romanesque manner, their caps and bases naturally being of stone. A number of sections suitable for columns about twelve and a half inches in diameter, are shown. Other examples of the treatment of piers and arches may be seen on pages seven, nine, eleven, fifty-one, fifty-three, and fifty-seven.

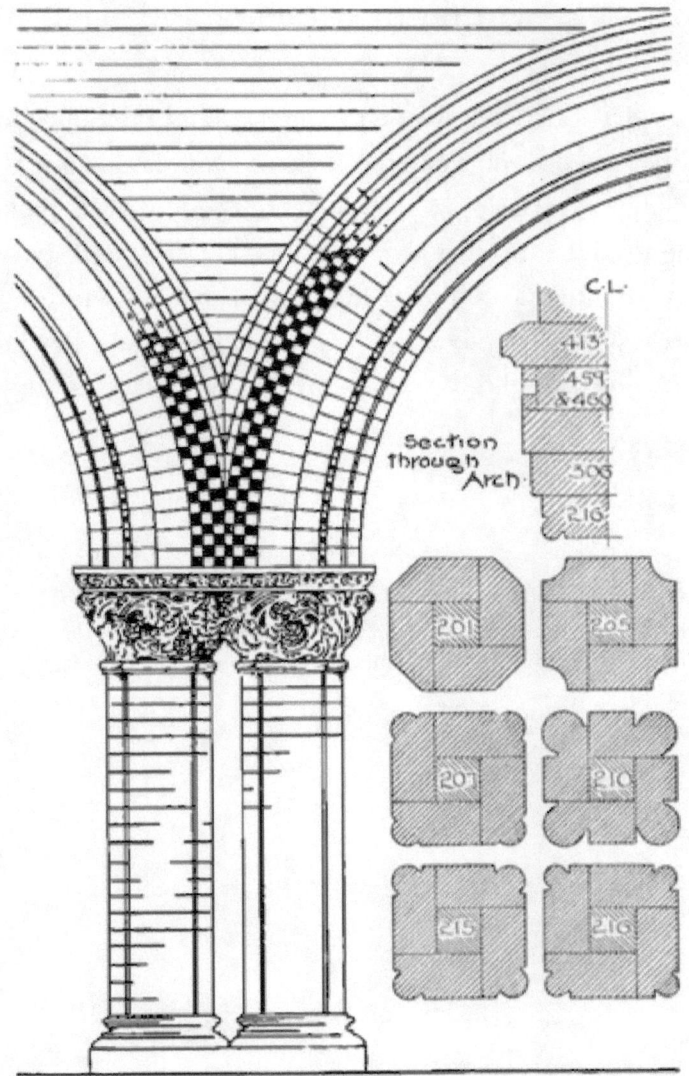

CIRCULAR PIERS

CIRCULAR piers, as suggested in the opposite drawing, may be built of various diameters, by using the radius bricks shown on page eighty-six. In this example the capitals and base are of stone. Other examples of columns bearing arches may be seen on pages seven, nine, eleven, fifty-one, fifty-three, and fifty-five.

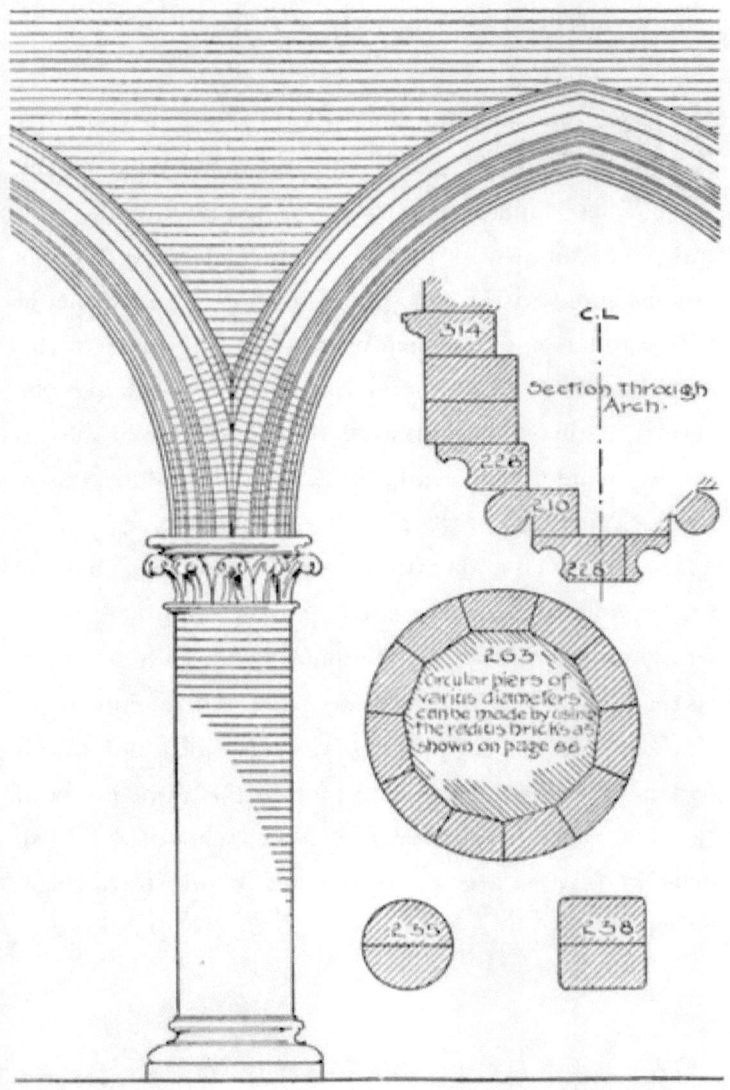

GATE POSTS AND WALL PIERS

IN the opposite illustration are given some examples of gate posts and posts used as the termination of walls. The panel of the central post is shown as having stone corners, but this is not essential to the design, as brick No. 442 is made with internal mitres, which may be used in place of the stone corners. The method of forming sunk panels, shown in this illustration, is, of course, applicable to the enrichment of wall surfaces as well as posts. Bricks Nos. 205, 218, 229, 406, 407, 410, 411, 430, 442, 463, 713, and 750 are well suited for use as the moulding of such sunk panels, and are made with internal mitres. The pier to the left is about sixteen inches wide, and six feet six inches high. The central pier is about two feet wide, and seven feet nine inches high. The pier to the right is about two feet wide, and seven feet nine inches high. The urns and balls are, of course, of stone, terra-cotta, or wood.

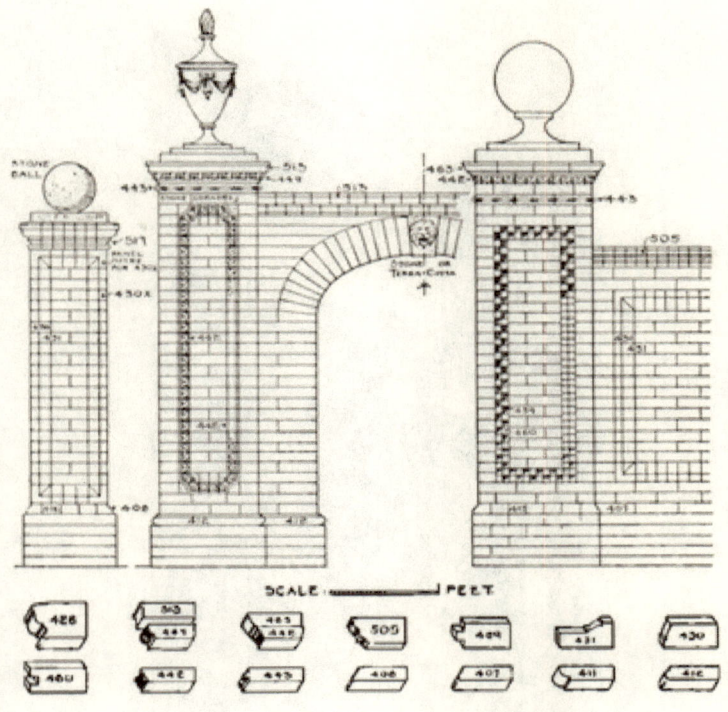

INDEX TO BRICK NUMBERS

BRICK	PAGE	BRICK	PAGE	BRICK	PAGE
201	72	217	76	233	78
202	72	218	76	234	78
203	72	220	76	235	80
204	72	221	76	236	80
205	72	223	69	237	80
207	72	226	178	238	80
210	74	228	78	240	82
211	74	229	78	241	82
212	74	230	78	242	82
215	74	231	78	243	82
216	76	232	78	245	82

INDEX TO BRICK NUMBERS

CONTINUED

BRICK	PAGE	BRICK	PAGE	BRICK	PAGE
246	82	305	92	402	120
260	86	306	92	403	120
261	86	308	94	404	120
262	86	309	94	405	120
263	86	310	94	406	120
264	86	311	94	407	120
265	86	312	96	408	120
266	86	313	96	410	120
267	86	314	96	411	122
268	86	315	96	412	122
269	86	316	98	413	122
270	86	317	98	414	122
271	86	318	98	415	122
272	86	319	98	416	124
273	86	320	100	417	124
274	86	321	100	418	124
275	86	322	100	419	148
277	86	323	100	420	148
280	86	351	106	426	148
281	86	352	106	430	112
283	86	353	106	430X	112
290	86	354	106	431	112
291	86	355	108	433	114
298	86	356	108	434	114
301	90	357	108	440	126
302	90	380	86	441	126
303	90	381	86	442	126
304	92	395	86	443	126

INDEX TO BRICK NUMBERS

CONTINUED

BRICK	PAGE	BRICK	PAGE	BRICK	PAGE
445	128	488	118	710	158
447	128	489	118	713	158
449	128	490	118	714	160
451	130	491	118	723	160
452	130	499	132	724	160
453	130	500	102 & 144	724R	160
455	132	501	102 & 144	726	162
457	132	502	102	727	162
459	134	503	102 & 144	728	162
460	134	504	102	729	164
463	136	505	144	730	164
465	136	506	104 & 144	731	166
466	136	507	104	732	166
467	136	508	104 & 144	733	166
468	136	509	104	734	68
471	138	510	146	750	168
472	138	511	146	750R	168
473	138	512	146	751	168
474	138	513	146	751R	168
475	138	514	146	802	170
477	136	518	152	813	170
480	140	519	152	814	172
481	140	520	152	915	174
484	140	521	152	916	174
485	118	522	152	917	176
486	118	603	158	918	176
487	118	606	158		

SERIES A

STANDARD AND ROMAN BRICKS

OWING to different shrinkage in clays, bricks made by the various companies differ in size, and different colors made by the same companies *may* vary in size.

Standard size, 8 to $8\frac{1}{8}$ x 4 to $4\frac{1}{4}$ x $2\frac{3}{16}$ to $2\frac{3}{8}$.

Roman size, $11\frac{1}{4}$ to $11\frac{3}{4}$ x 4 to $4\frac{1}{4}$ x $1\frac{1}{2}$ to $1\frac{11}{16}$.

Roman lengths can be made to order as thick as $2\frac{1}{2}$ inches.

PLAIN BLOCKS

These shrink in same proportion, and lay in the wall in even courses with standard size of same color and make.

No. 734. $9\frac{1}{2}$ to 10 x $4\frac{3}{4}$ to 5 x $2\frac{1}{2}$.

No. 223. 8 to $8\frac{1}{8}$ x 8 to $8\frac{1}{8}$ x $2\frac{3}{16}$ to $2\frac{3}{8}$.

No. 601. $4\frac{3}{4}$ to 5 x 4 to $4\frac{1}{4}$ x $2\frac{1}{2}$.

No. 602. $4\frac{3}{4}$ to 5 x $4\frac{3}{4}$ to 5 x $2\frac{1}{2}$.

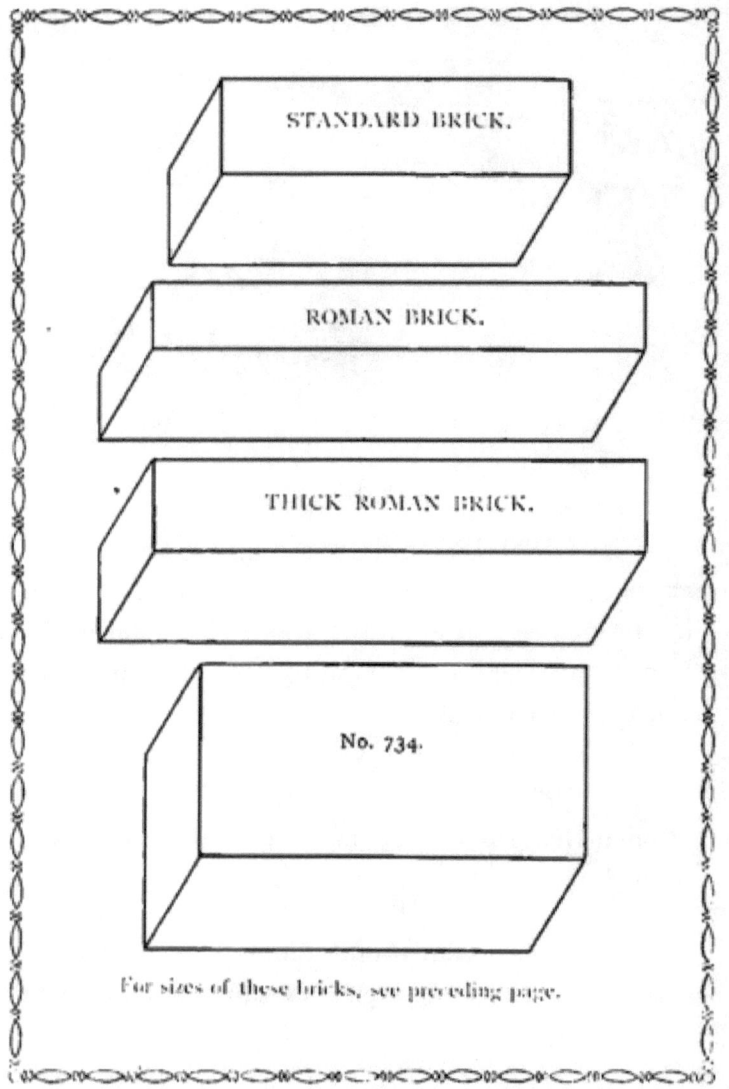

For sizes of these bricks, see preceding page.

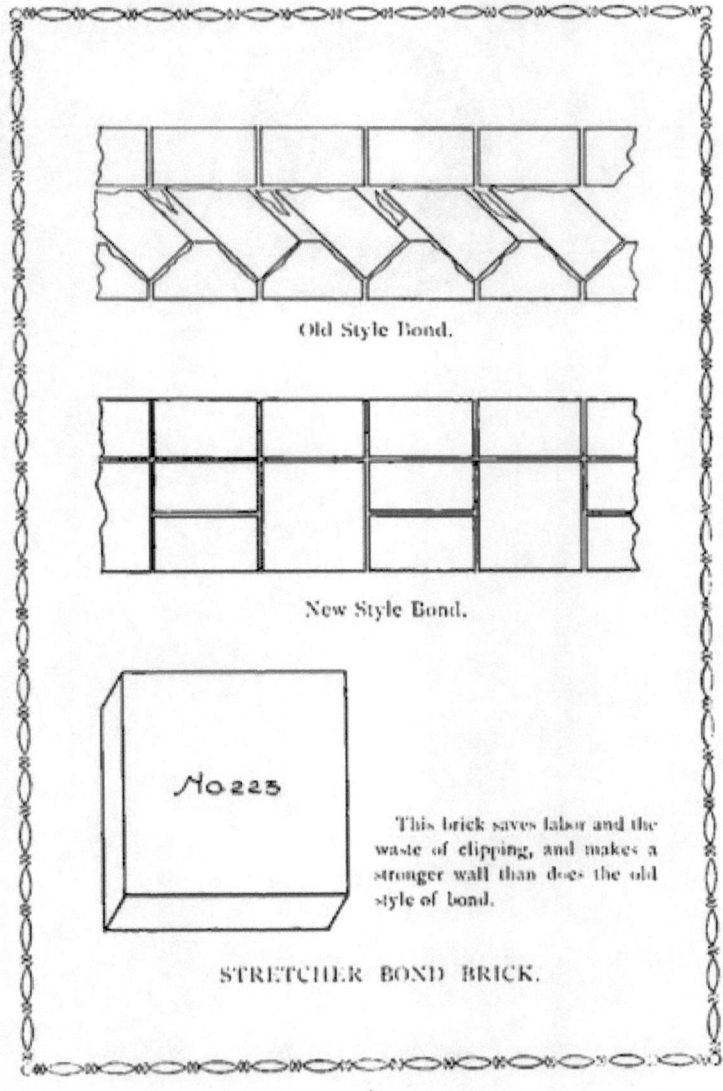

Old Style Bond.

New Style Bond.

This brick saves labor and the waste of clipping, and makes a stronger wall than does the old style of bond.

STRETCHER BOND BRICK.

SERIES B

ANGLE BRICKS, JAMB AND ARCH MOULDINGS

MANY of the bricks shown in this series are particularly suitable for use in angles of buildings. This is especially true of Nos. 211 and 212, which can be used to turn an angle of any number of degrees. Other bricks suitable for use in jambs and arches may be found in Series D, E, G, and K. Many of the bricks included in this section and Section D are useful in forming piers, as shown on page fifty-nine.

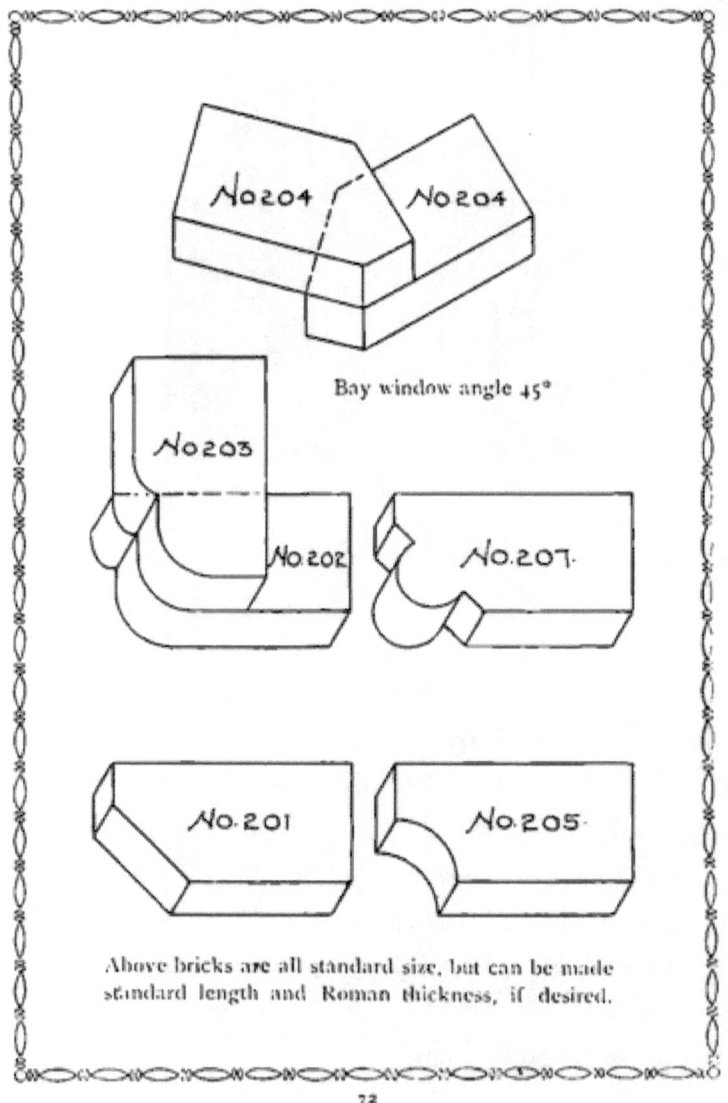

Bay window angle 45°

Above bricks are all standard size, but can be made standard length and Roman thickness, if desired.

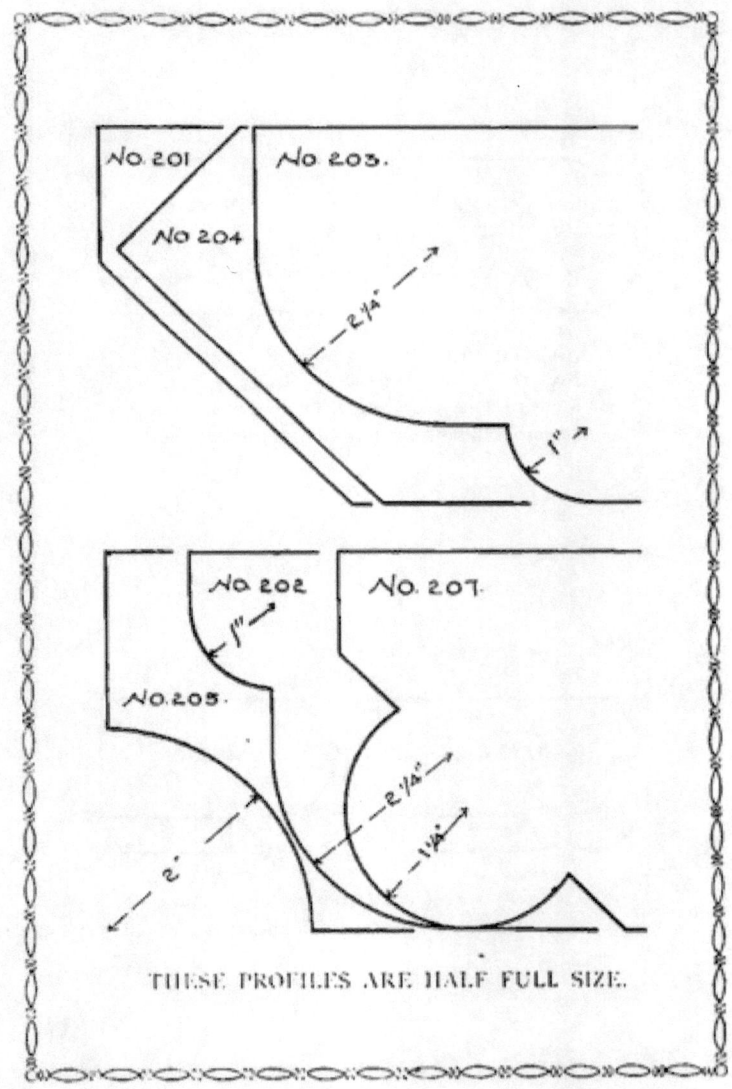

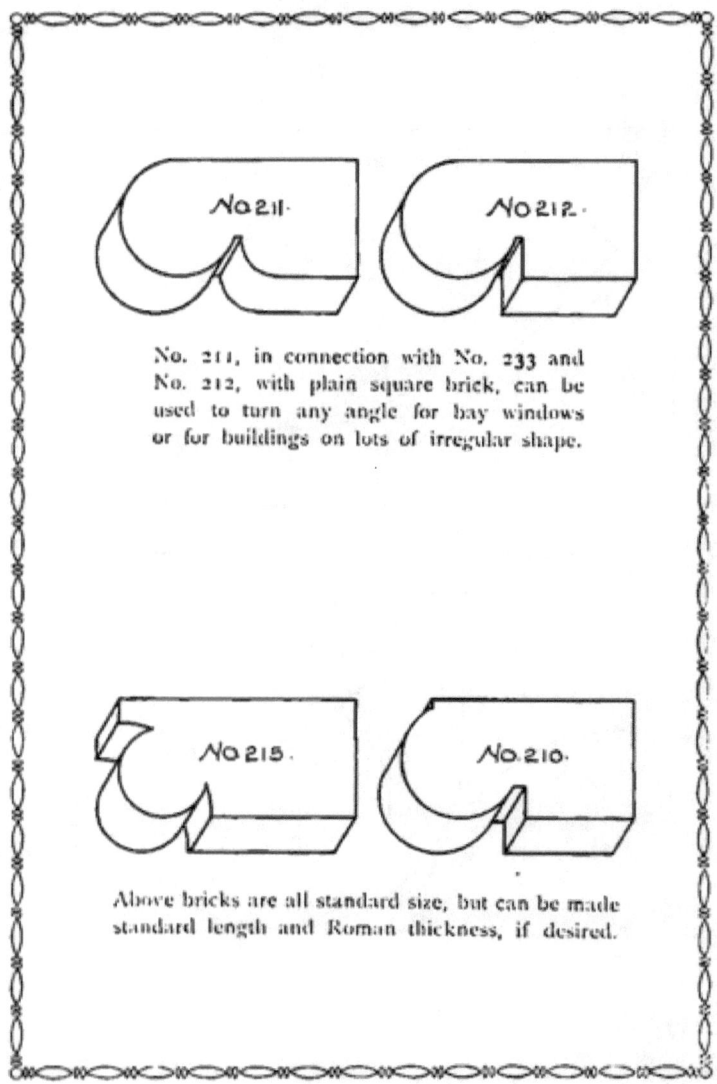

No. 211, in connection with No. 233 and No. 212, with plain square brick, can be used to turn any angle for bay windows or for buildings on lots of irregular shape.

Above bricks are all standard size, but can be made standard length and Roman thickness, if desired.

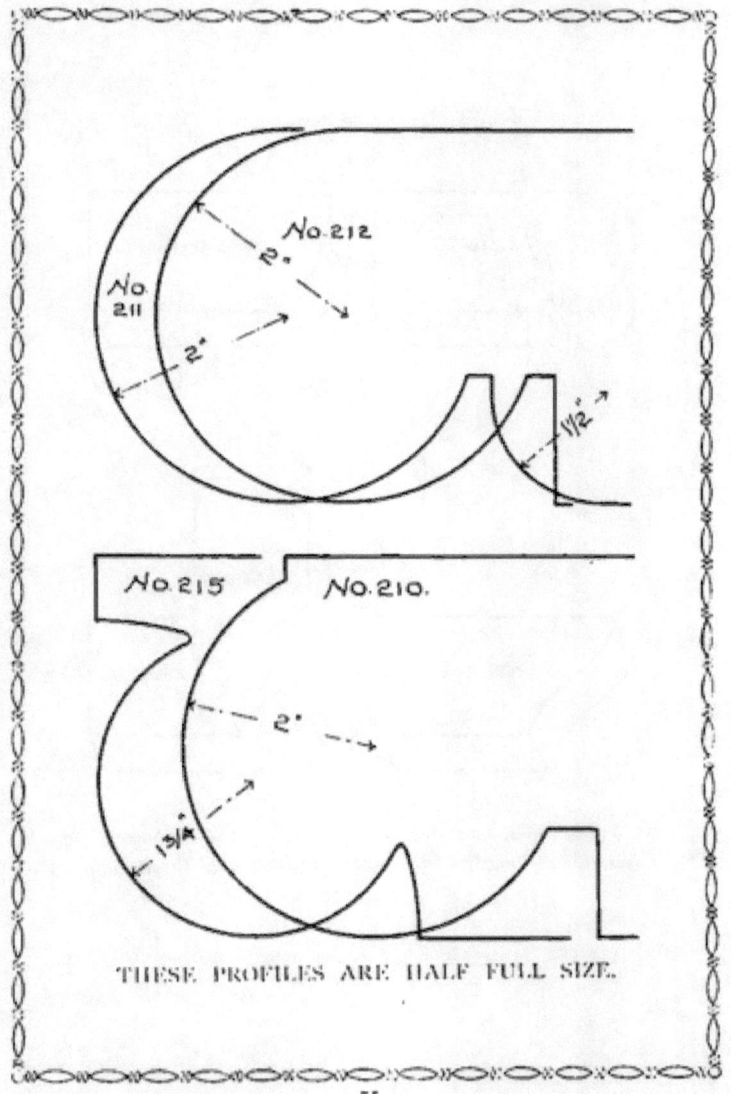

THESE PROFILES ARE HALF FULL SIZE.

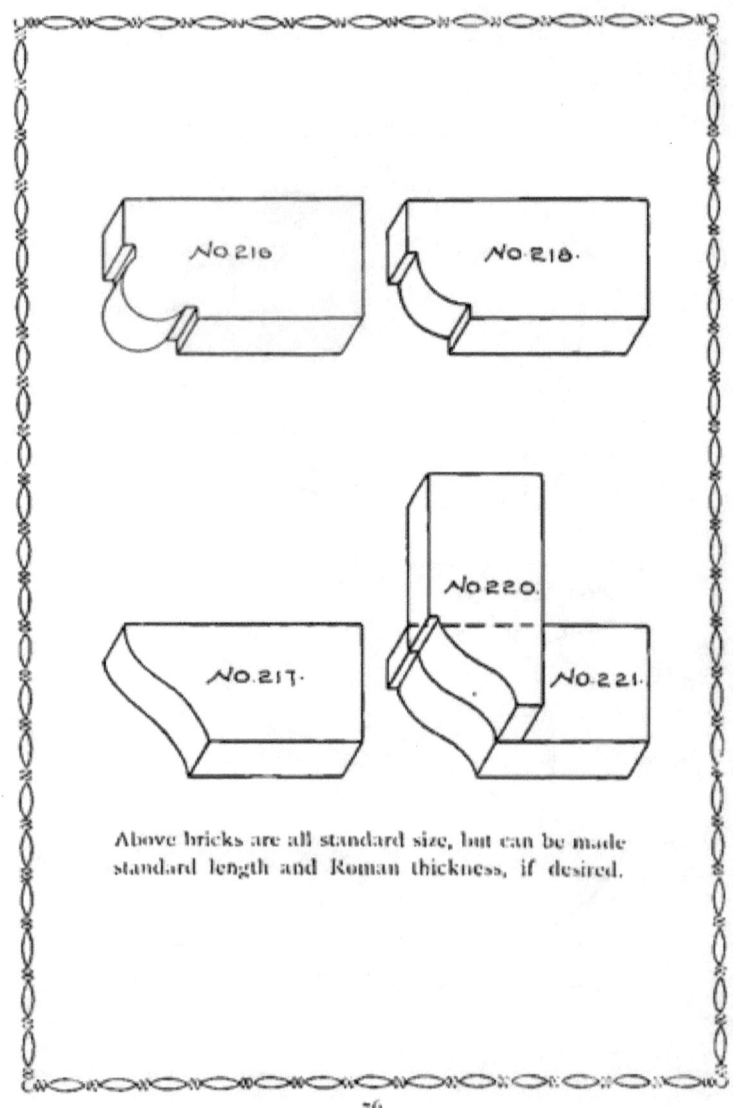

Above bricks are all standard size, but can be made standard length and Roman thickness, if desired.

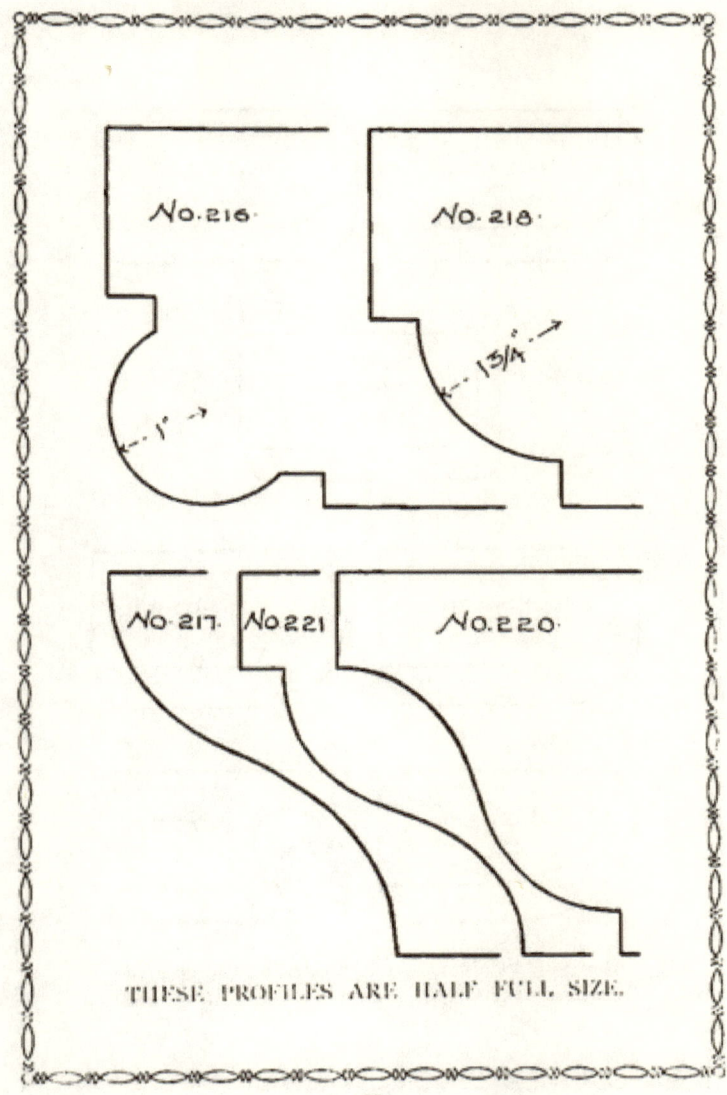

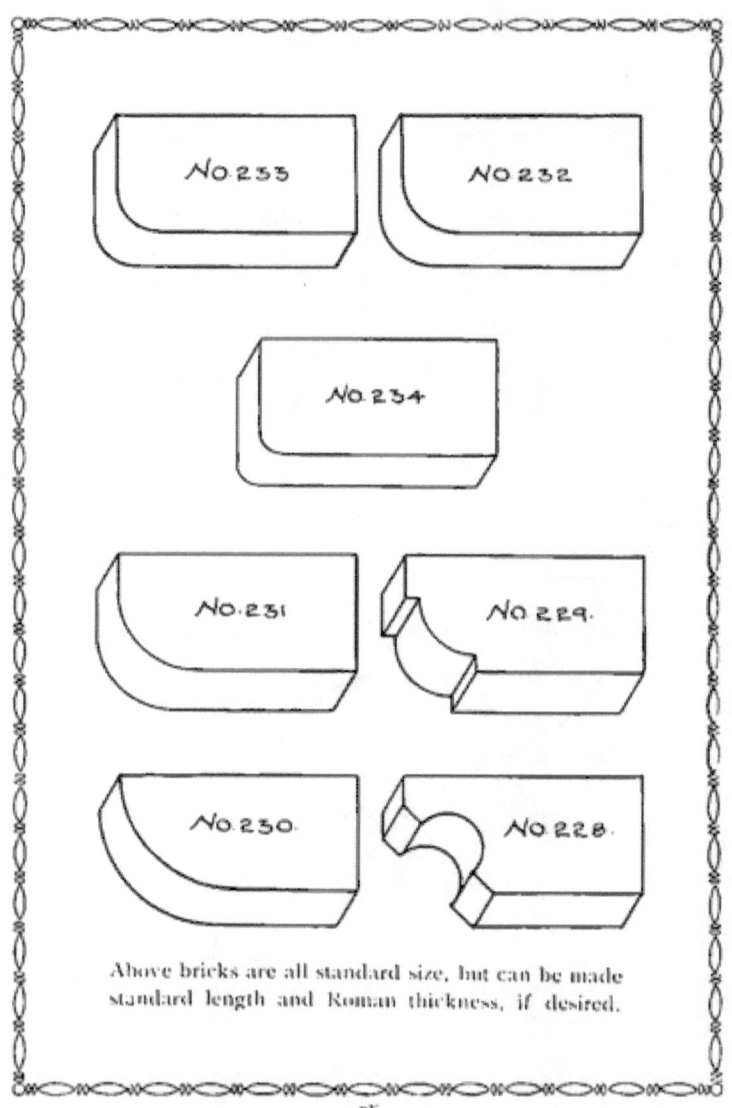

Above bricks are all standard size, but can be made standard length and Roman thickness, if desired.

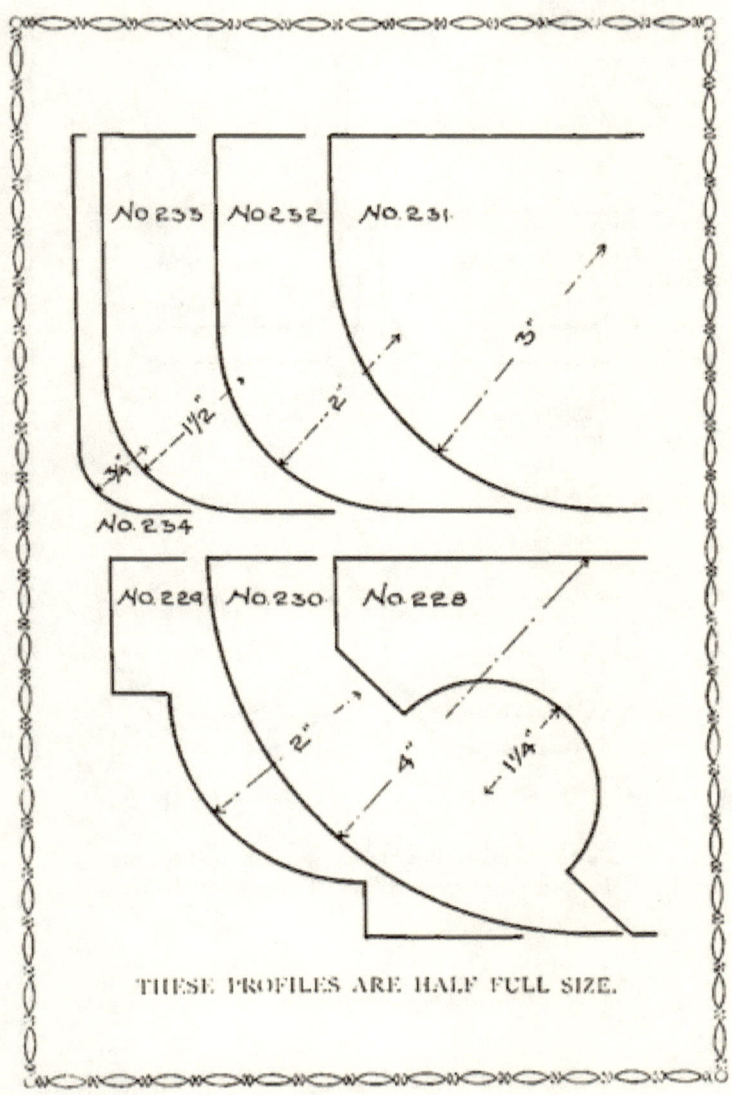

THESE PROFILES ARE HALF FULL SIZE.

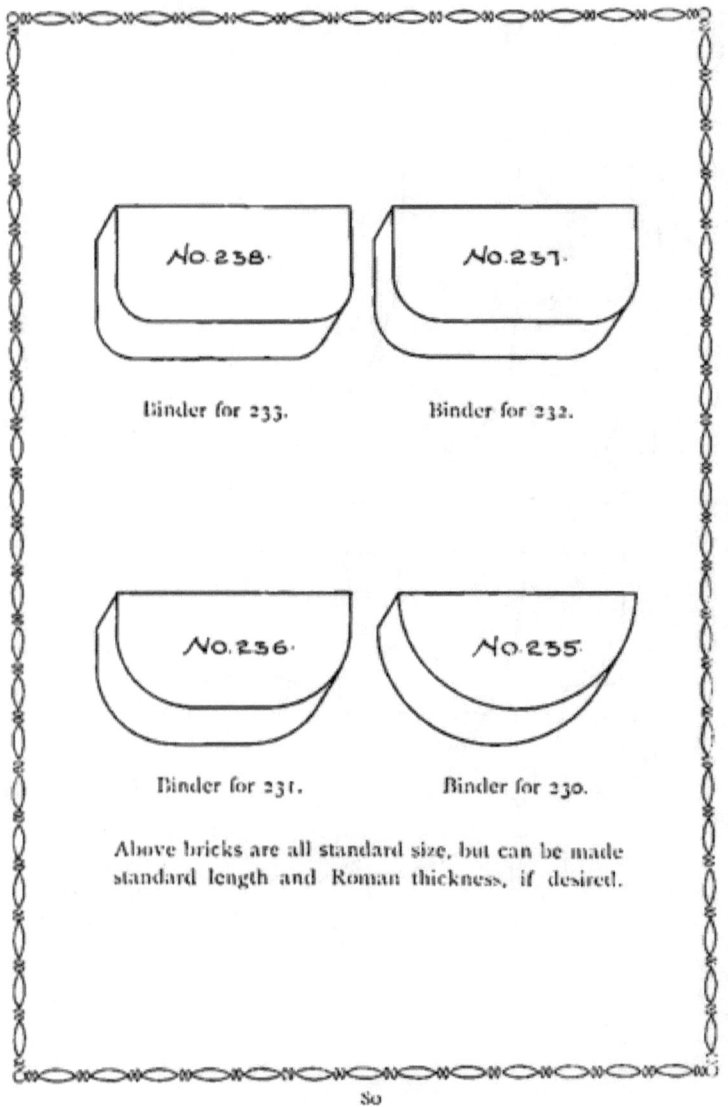

Above bricks are all standard size, but can be made standard length and Roman thickness, if desired.

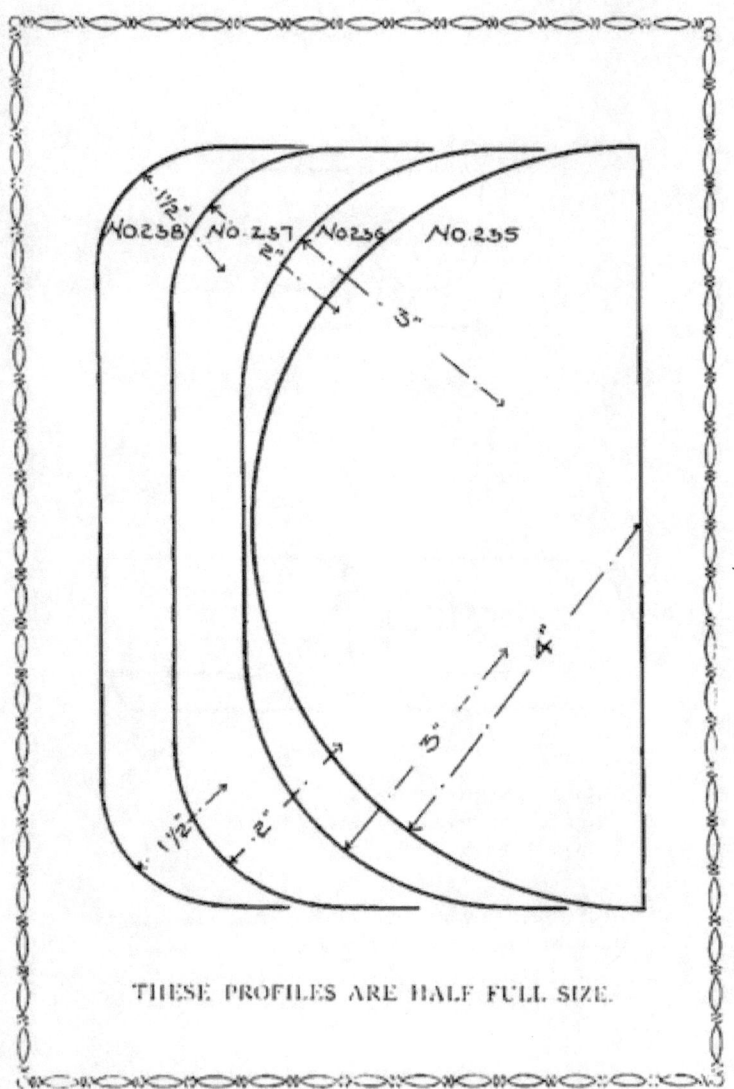

THESE PROFILES ARE HALF FULL SIZE.

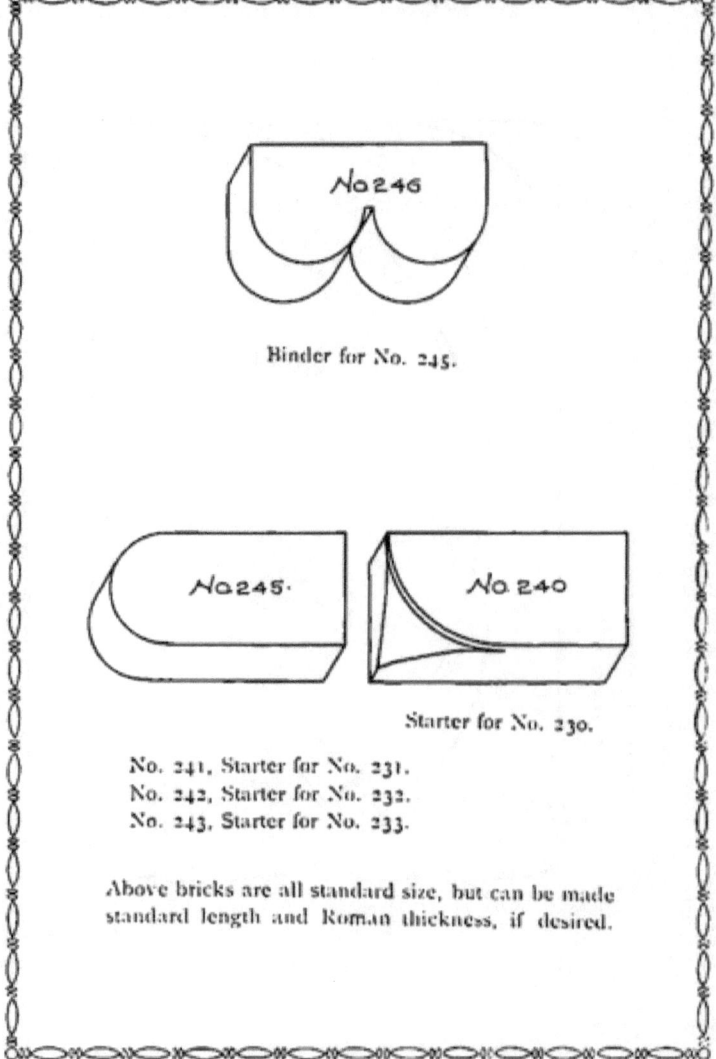

Binder for No. 245.

Starter for No. 230.

No. 241, Starter for No. 231.
No. 242, Starter for No. 232.
No. 243, Starter for No. 233.

Above bricks are all standard size, but can be made standard length and Roman thickness, if desired.

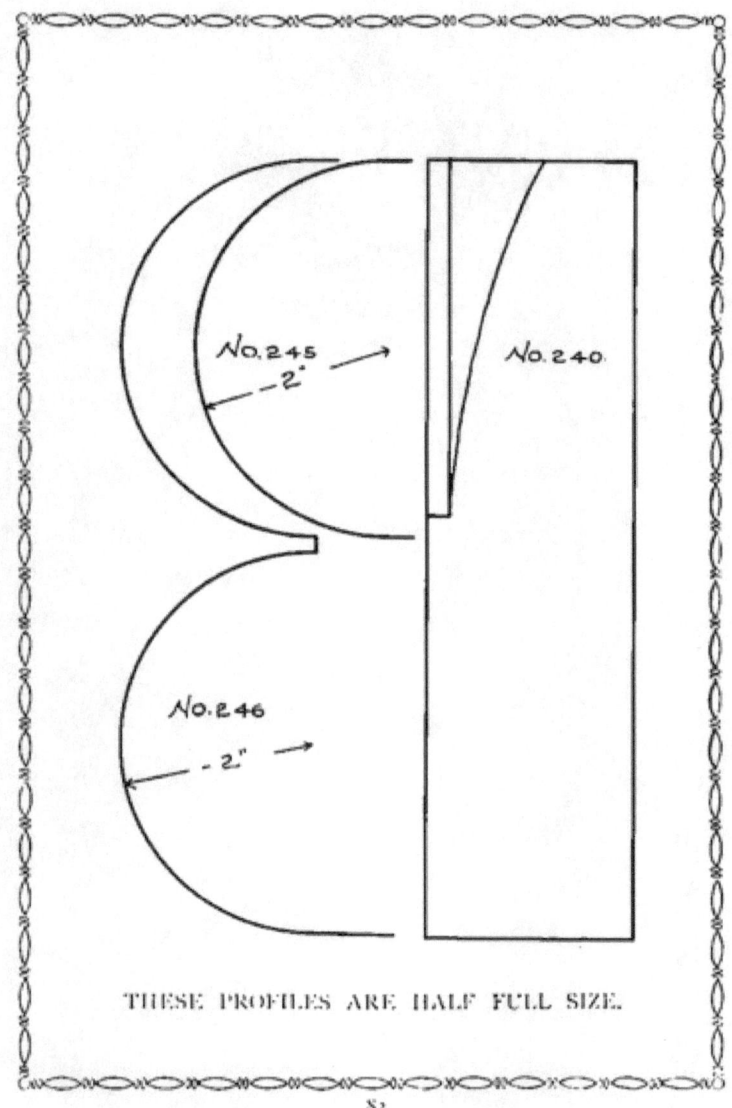

SERIES C
RADIUS BRICKS

CIRCULAR work, as in a column, pier, or exterior of an apse or tower, may be built of any radius greater than four and a half inches with the bricks shown in this section. For a radius greater than four feet, the several radii made are sufficiently close to each other to enable their use for any intermediate radius; for example, a brick of five feet seven inches radius can be used to turn a circle of either five feet or six feet radius. For radii over thirty feet, the brick become practically straight, and it is not necessary to make them in special moulds.

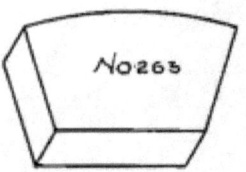

RADIUS BRICKS.

No. 270.— 4½ in. radius.　　No. 263.— 2 ft. 9 in. radius.
No. 275.— 5 in.　　"　　No. 277.— 3 ft. 0 in.　　"
No. 260.— 6 in.　　"　　No. 269.— 3 ft. 6 in.　　"
No. 291.— 7½ in.　　"　　No. 270.— 4 ft. 6 in.　　"
No. 261.— 8½ in.　　"　　No. 271.— 5 ft. 7 in.　　"
No. 262.—10 in.　　"　　No. 272.— 6 ft. 9 in.　　"
No. 263.—13 in.　　"　　No. 273.— 8 ft. 0 in.　　"
No. 264.—15 in.　　"　　No. 274.—10 ft. 0 in.　　"
No. 265.—18 in.　　"　　No. 380.—12 ft. 0 in.　　"
No. 266.—20 in.　　"　　No. 381.—16 ft. 0 in.　　"
No. 267.—24 in.　　"　　No. 395.—20 ft. 0 in.　　"

Nos. 380, 381, and 395 are Roman size.

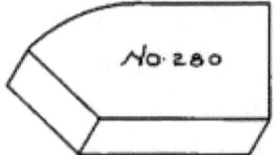

Starter for No. 260.—6 in. radius.

No. 298, Starter for No. 291.— 7½ in. radius.
No. 281, Starter for No. 261.— 8½ in.　　"
No. 283, Starter for No. 263.—13 in.　　"

Bricks from 4½ in. to 10 ft. radius are all standard size, but can be made standard length and Roman thickness.

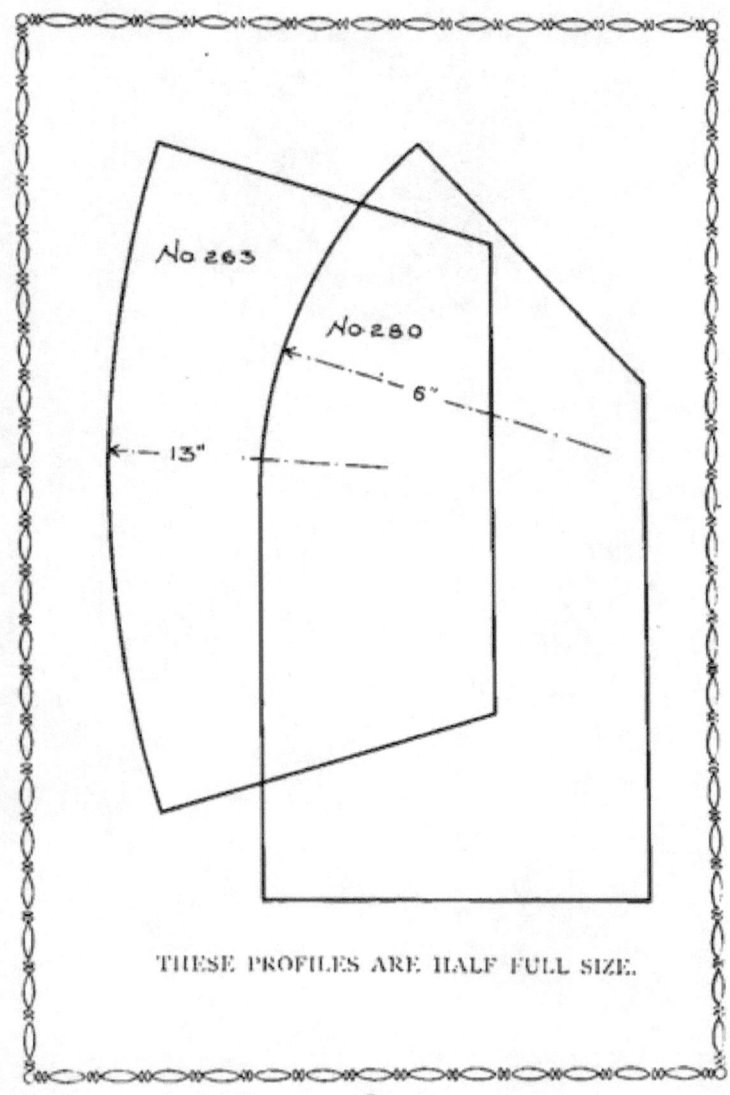

THESE PROFILES ARE HALF FULL SIZE.

SERIES D

JAMB AND ARCH MOULDINGS

THE bricks shown in this section are especially designed for use in jambs and arches. Other bricks suitable for these uses may be found in Series B, E, F, H, and K. Some combinations of such bricks may be seen on pages twenty-five and twenty-seven, and in the jambs of the windows, pages nineteen and twenty-one.

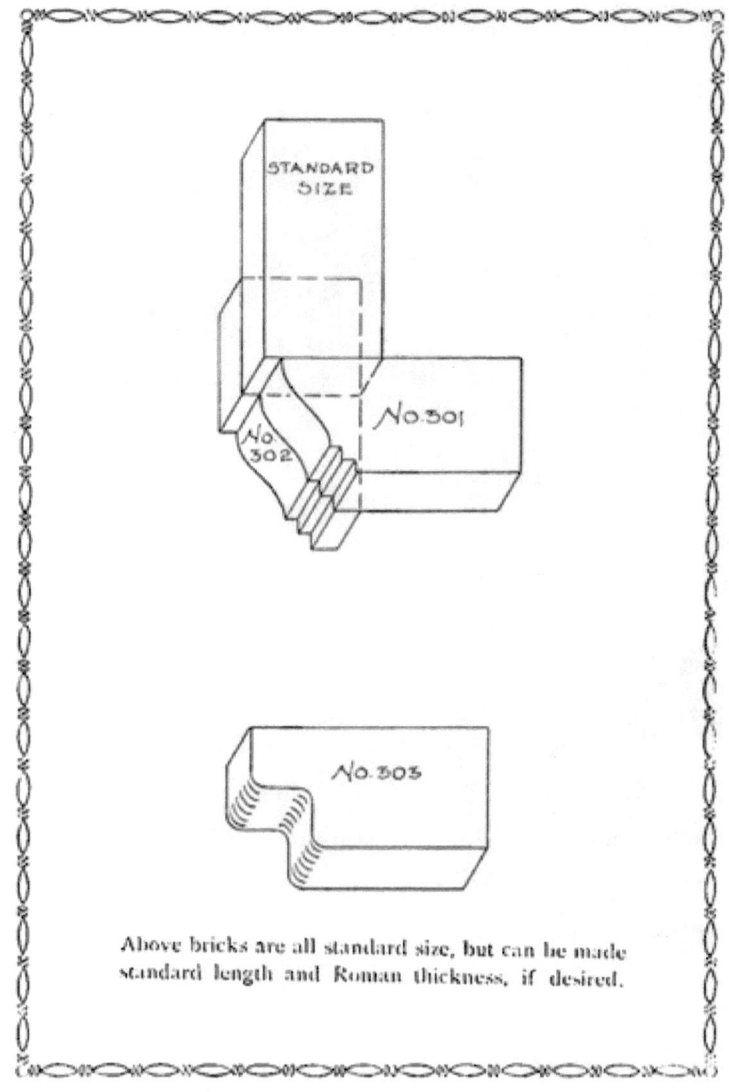

Above bricks are all standard size, but can be made standard length and Roman thickness, if desired.

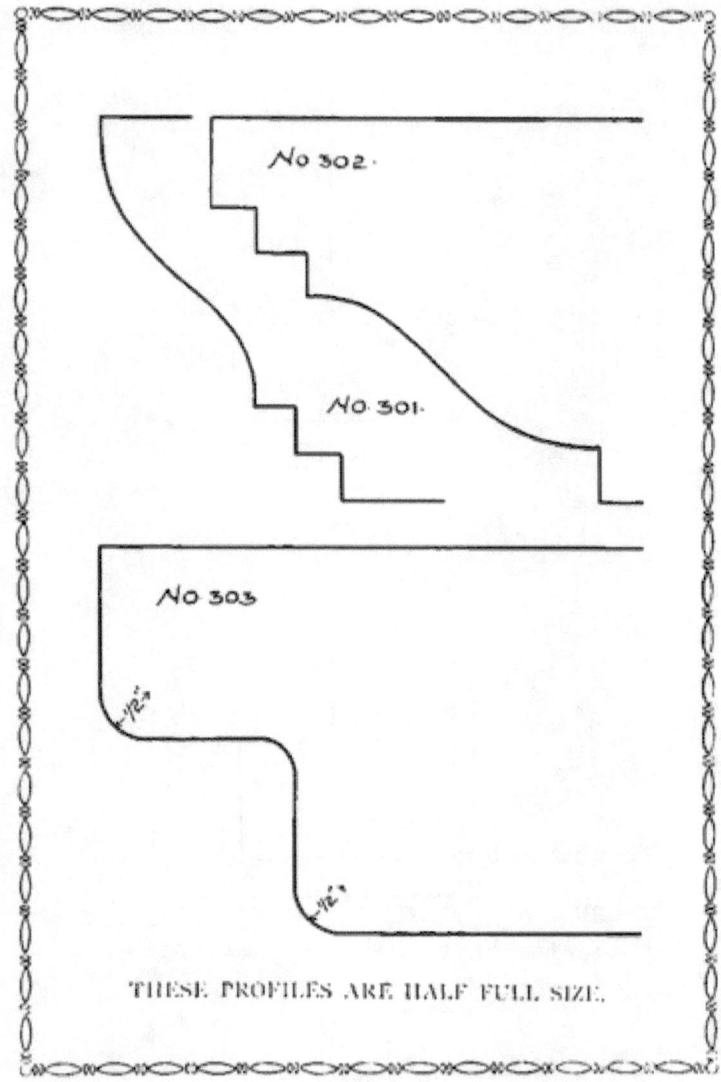

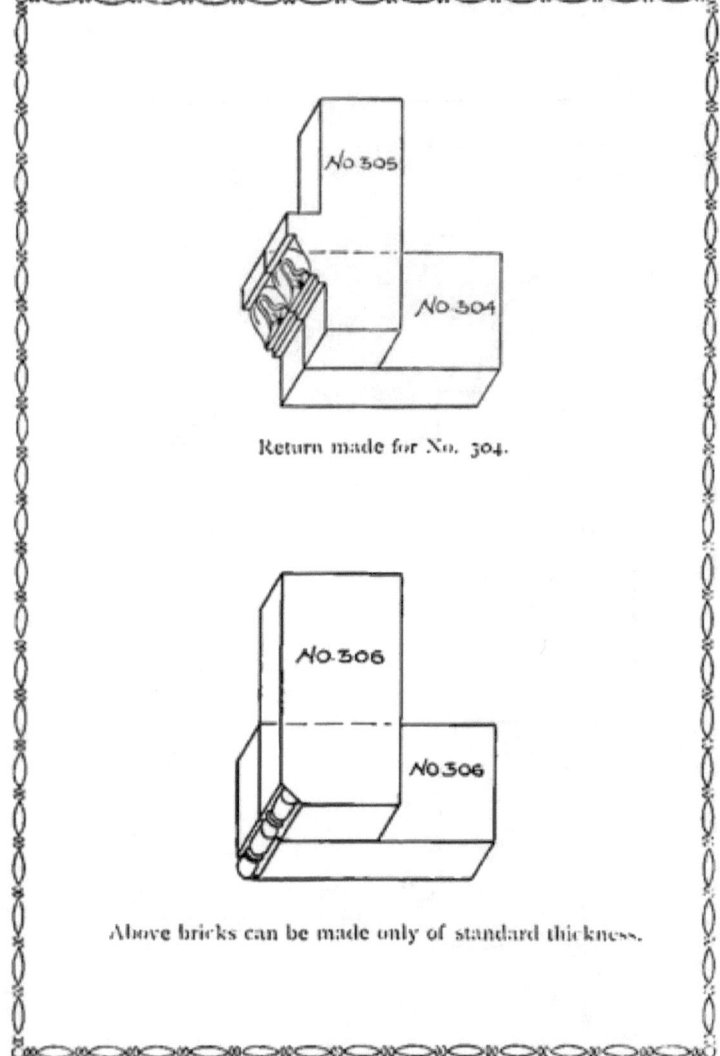

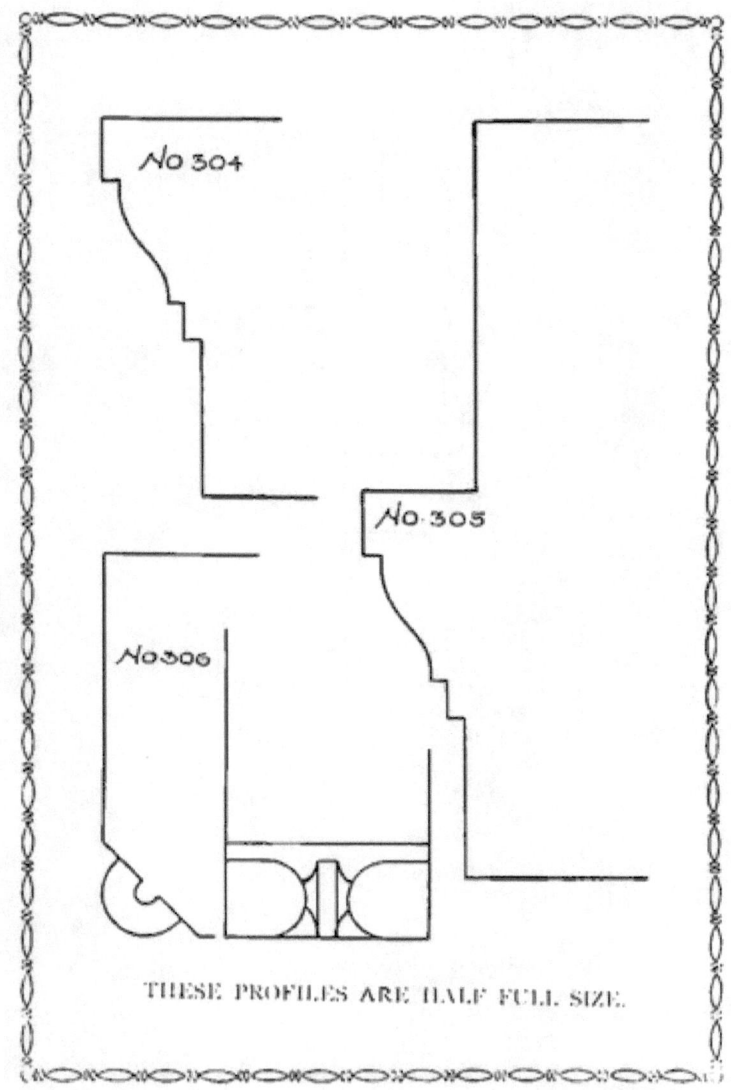

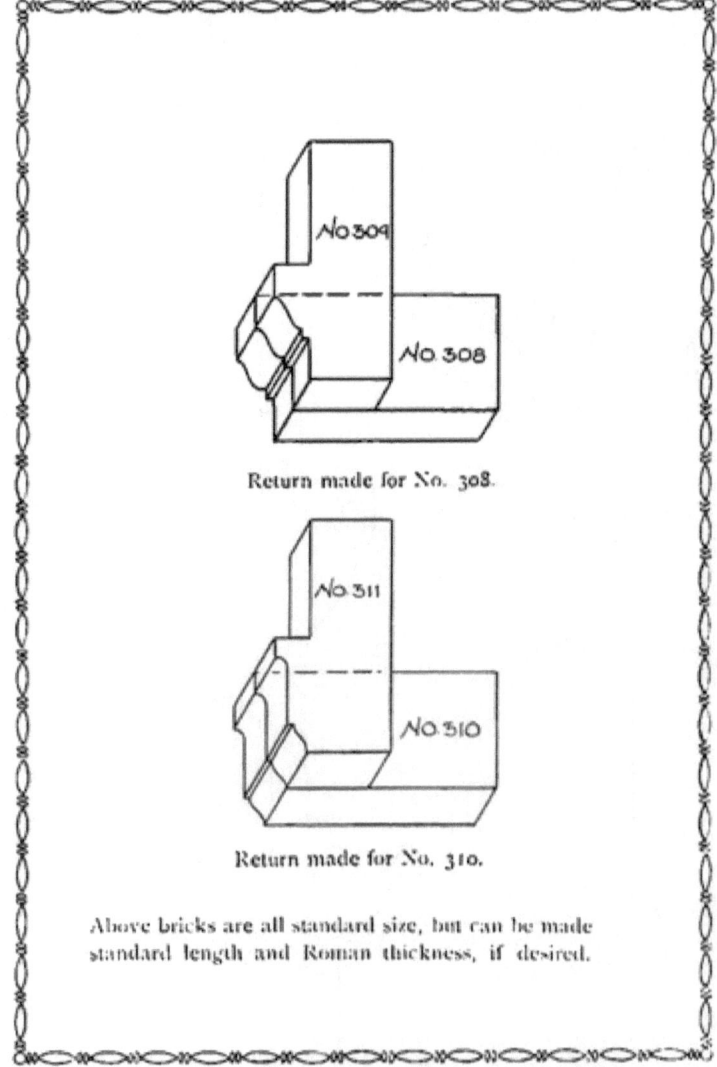

Return made for No. 308.

Return made for No. 310.

Above bricks are all standard size, but can be made standard length and Roman thickness, if desired.

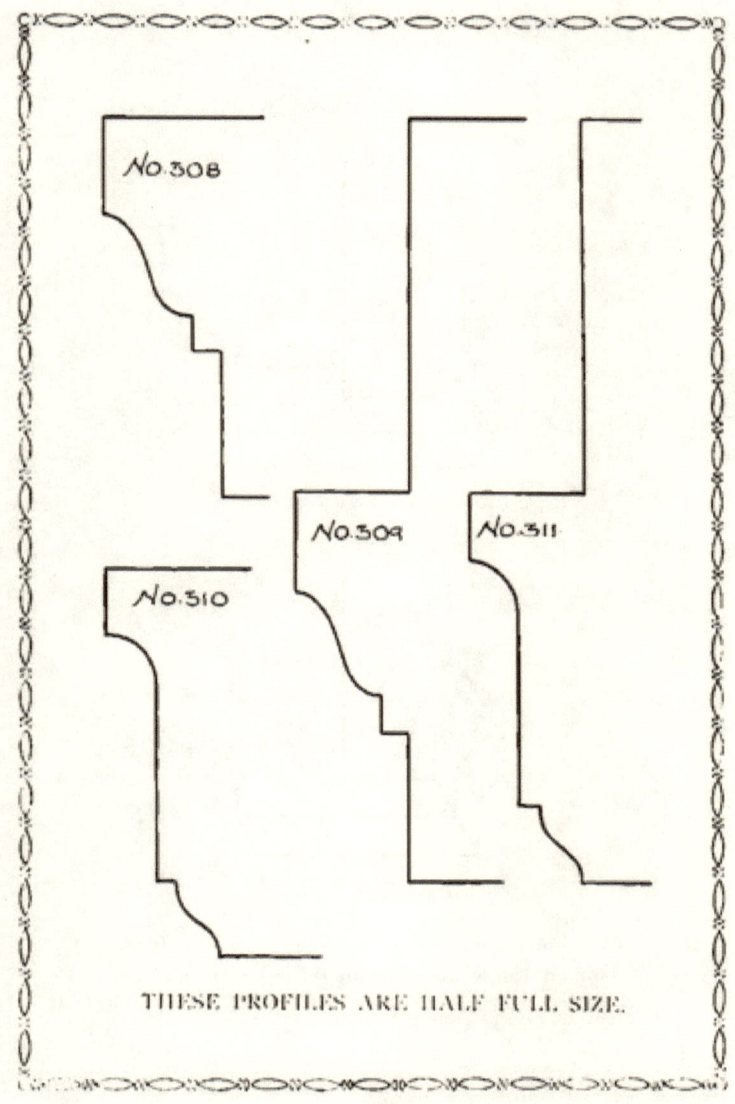

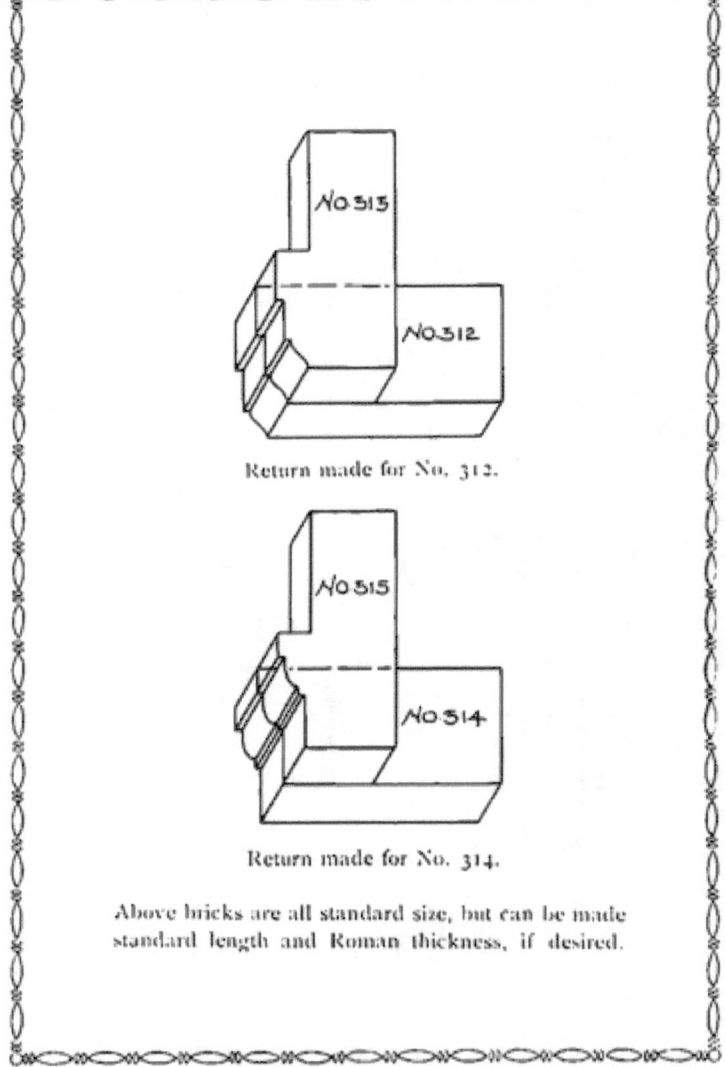

Return made for No. 312.

Return made for No. 314.

Above bricks are all standard size, but can be made standard length and Roman thickness, if desired.

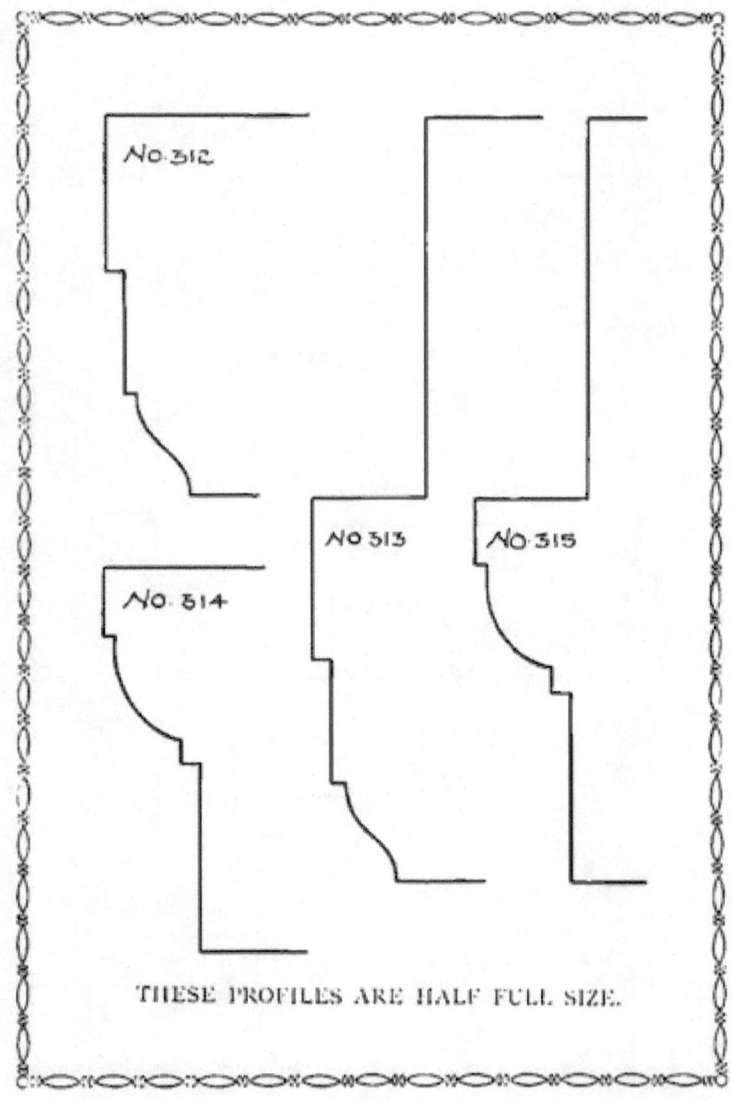

THESE PROFILES ARE HALF FULL SIZE.

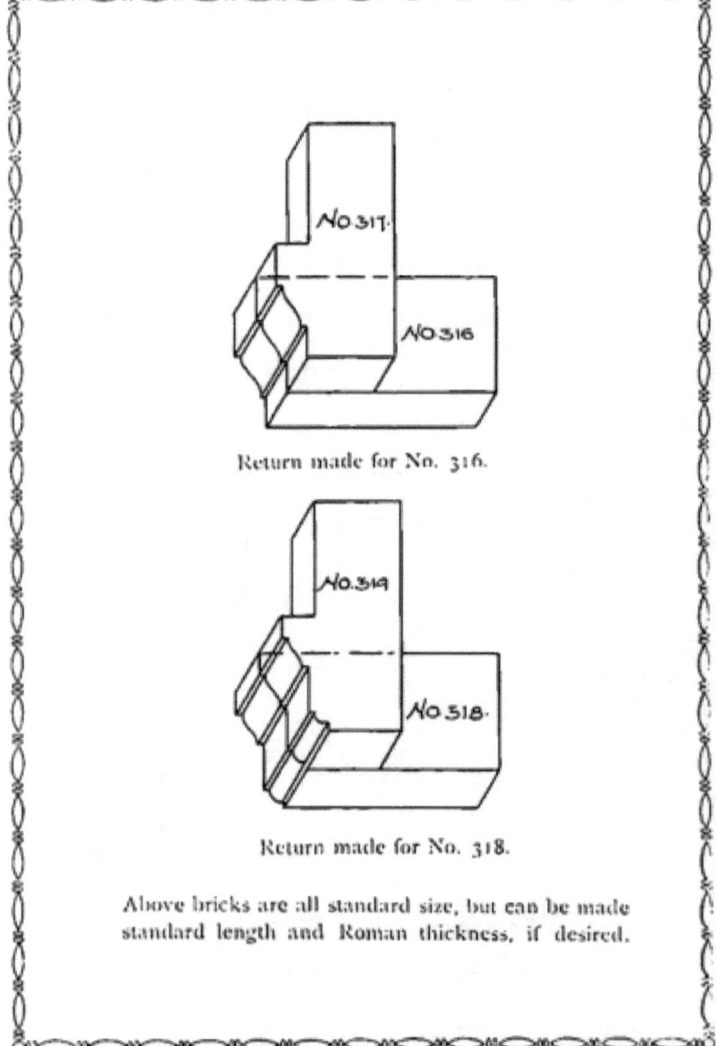

Return made for No. 316.

Return made for No. 318.

Above bricks are all standard size, but can be made standard length and Roman thickness, if desired.

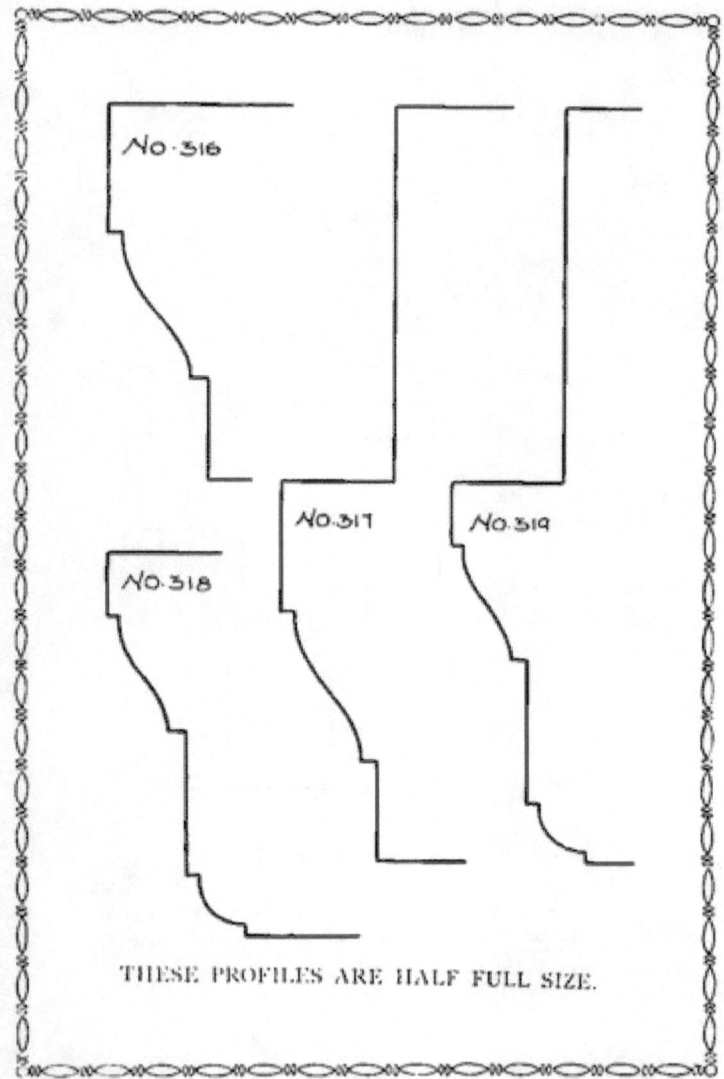

THESE PROFILES ARE HALF FULL SIZE.

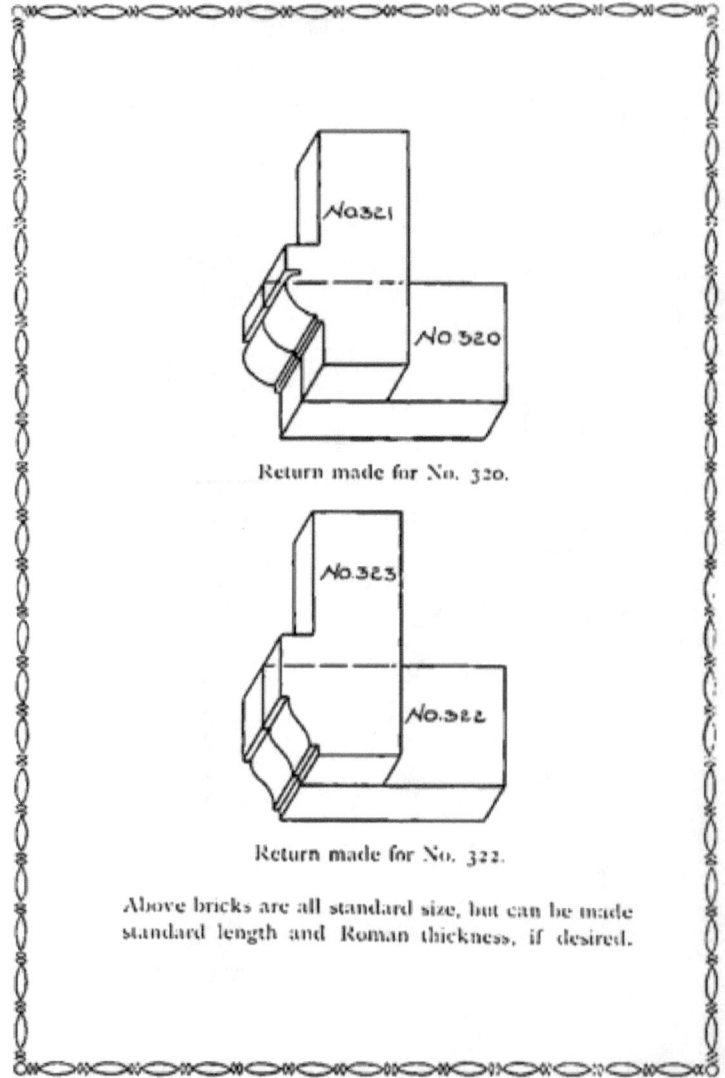

Return made for No. 320.

Return made for No. 322.

Above bricks are all standard size, but can be made standard length and Roman thickness, if desired.

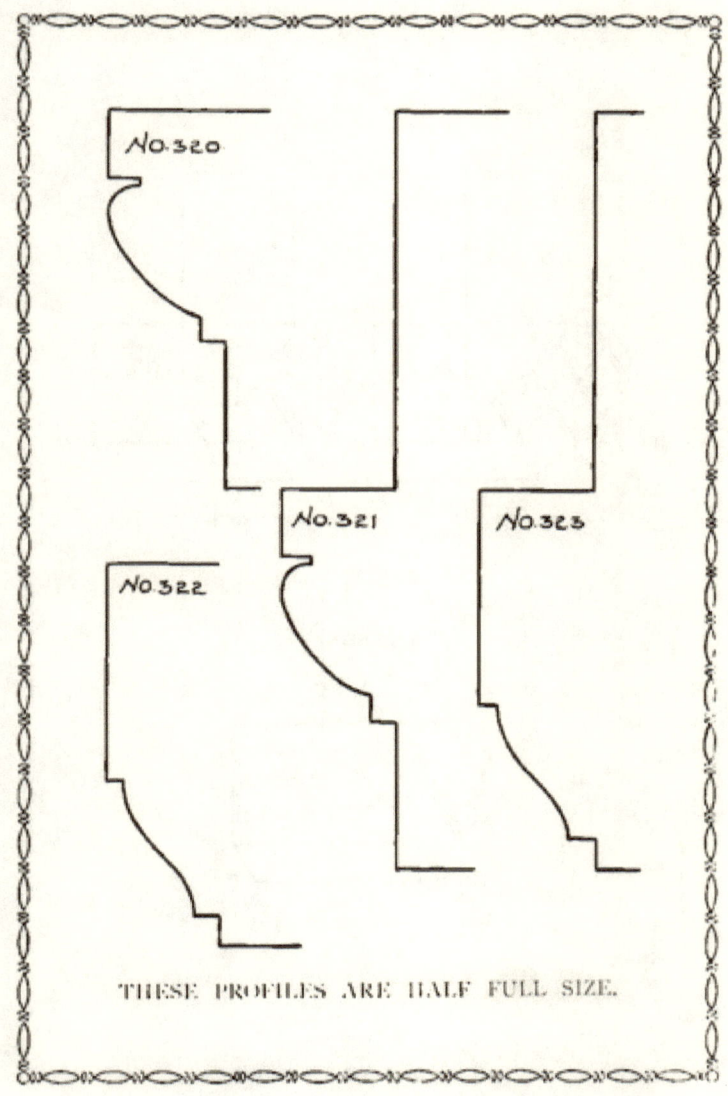

THESE PROFILES ARE HALF FULL SIZE.

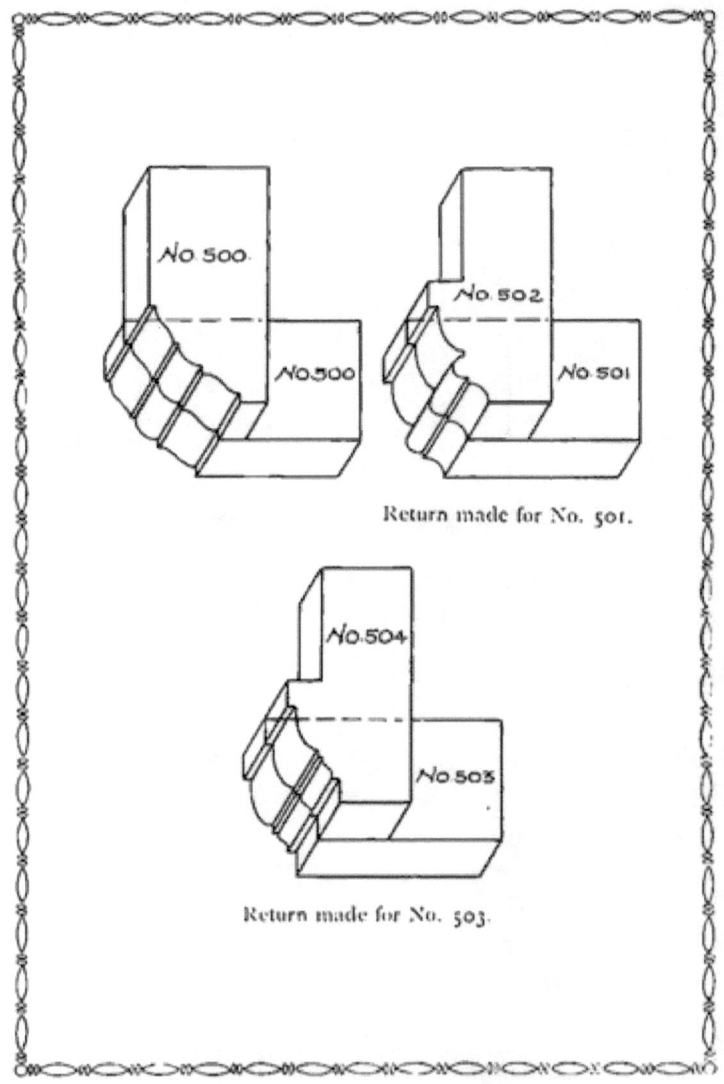

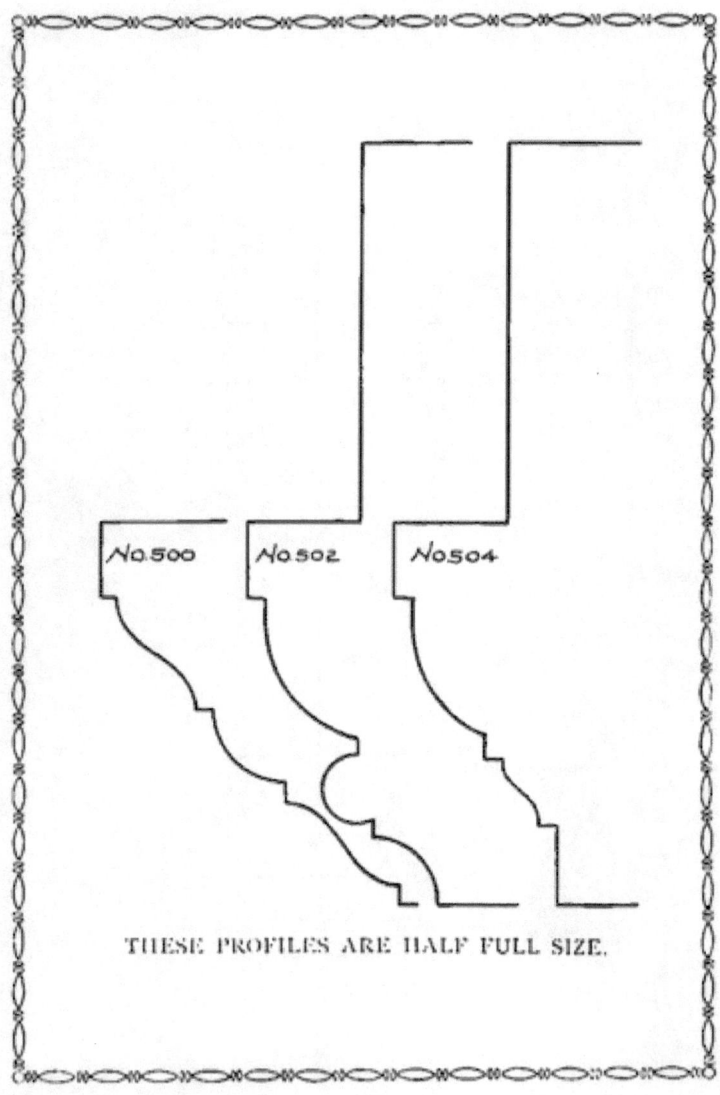

THESE PROFILES ARE HALF FULL SIZE.

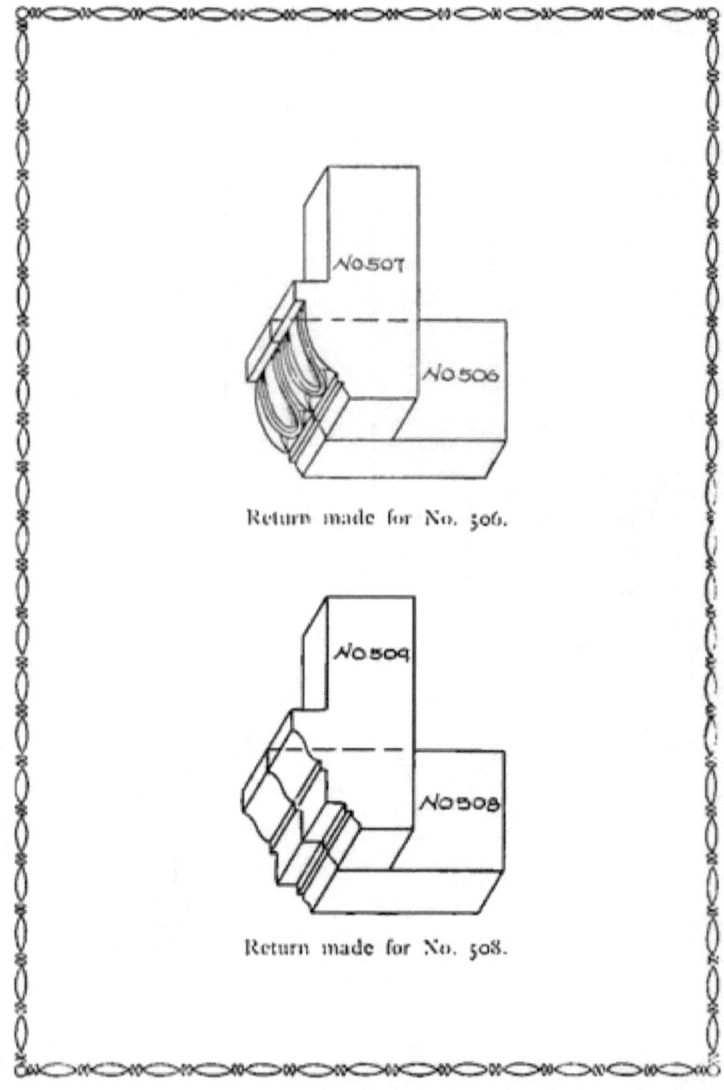

Return made for No. 506.

Return made for No. 508.

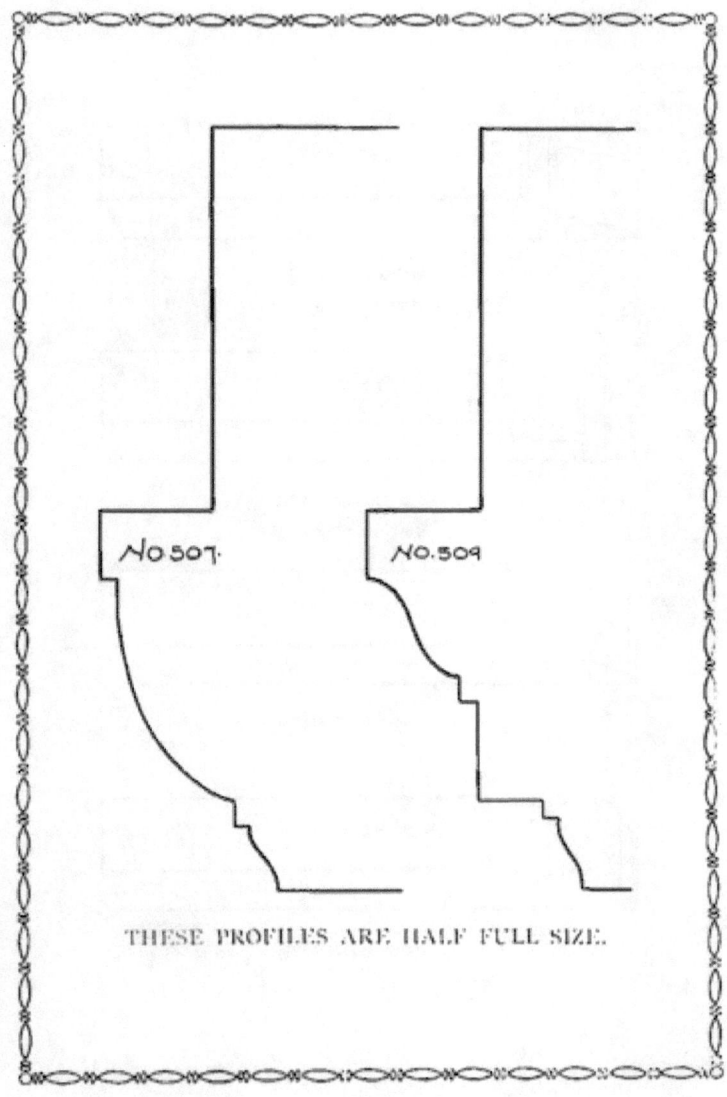

THESE PROFILES ARE HALF FULL SIZE.

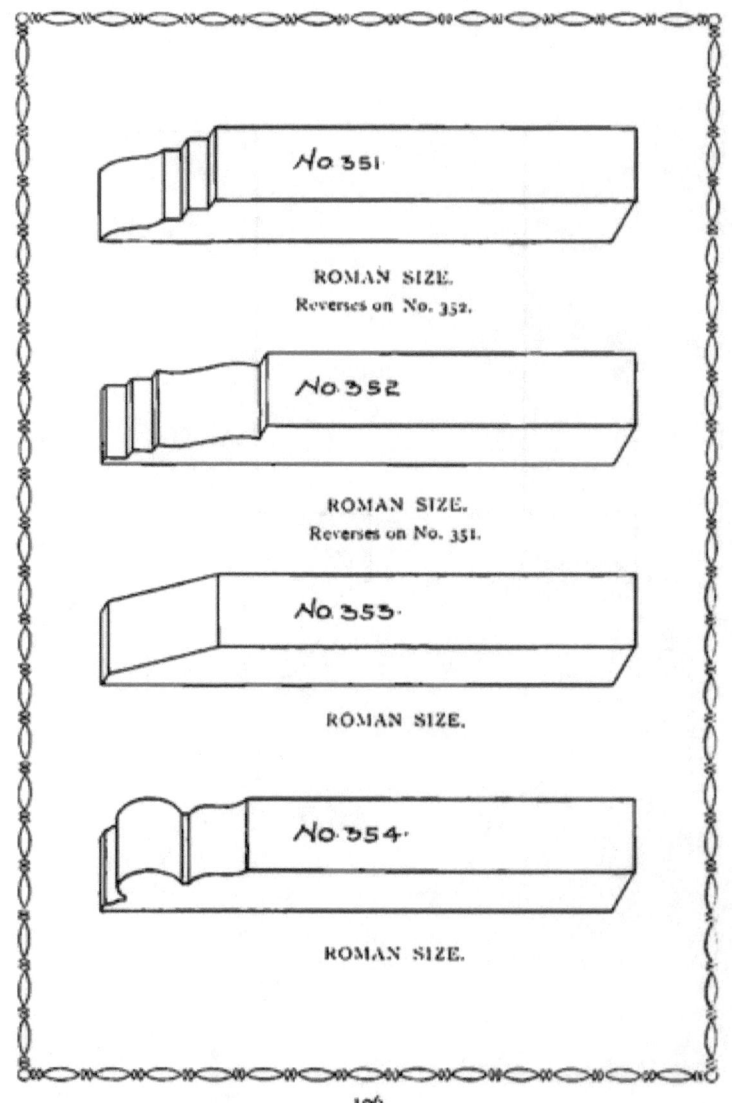

No. 351.

ROMAN SIZE.
Reverses on No. 352.

No. 352.

ROMAN SIZE.
Reverses on No. 351.

No. 353.

ROMAN SIZE.

No. 354.

ROMAN SIZE.

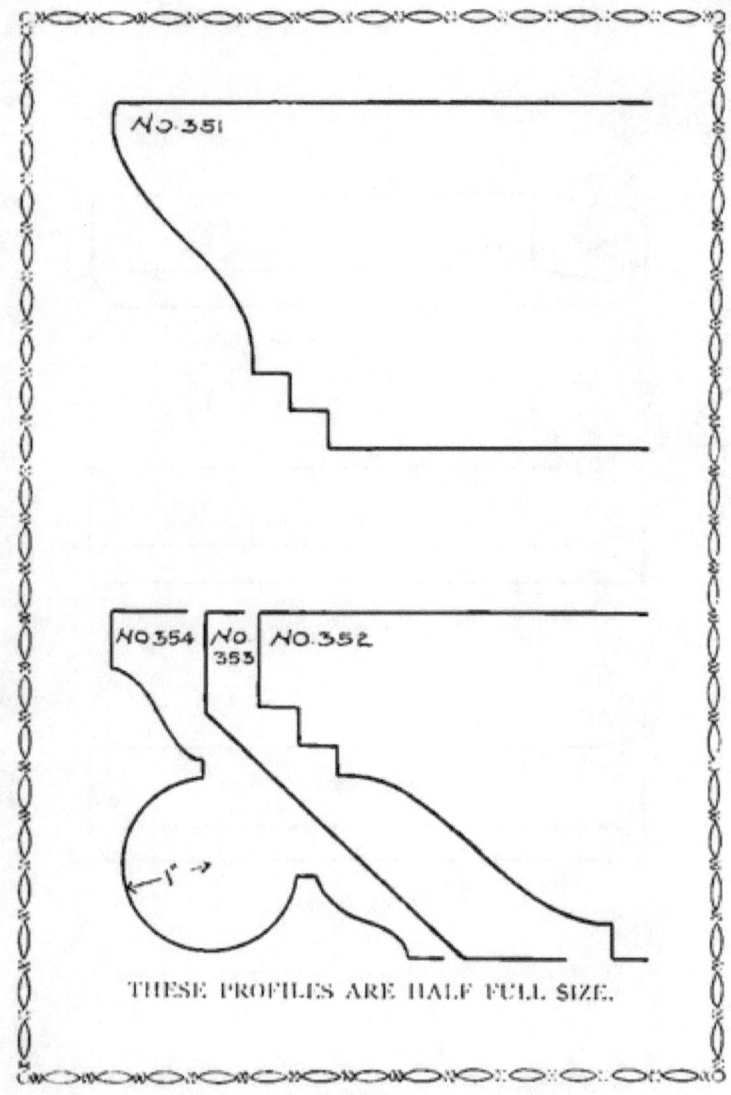

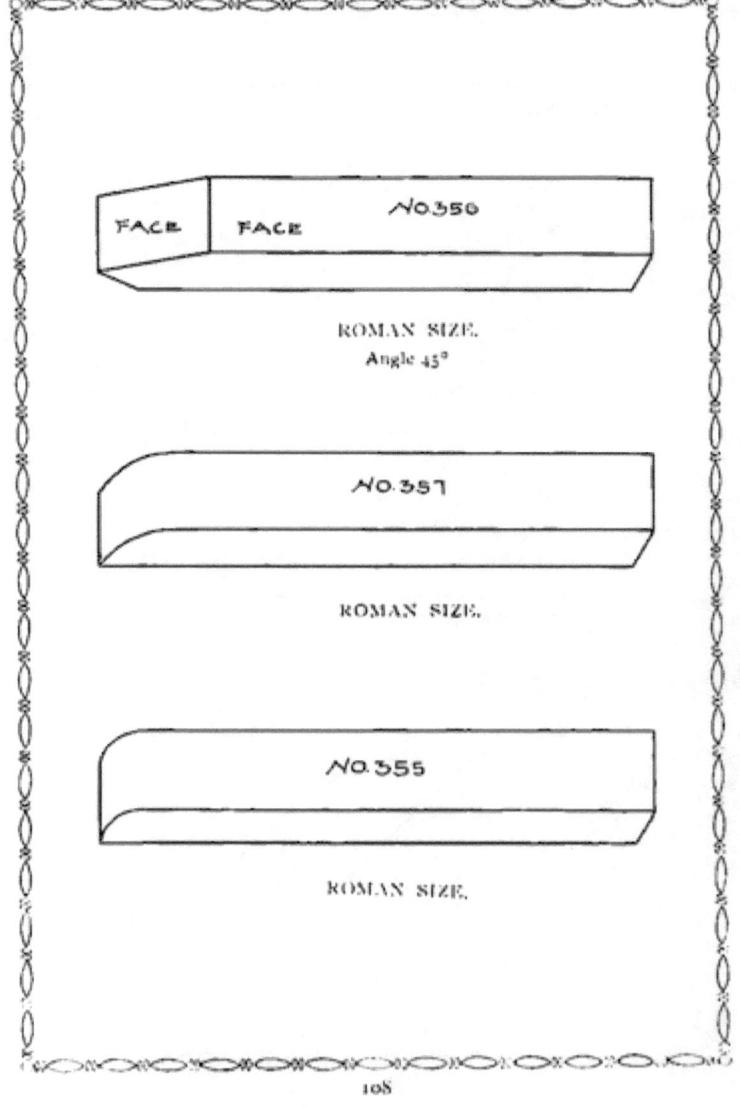

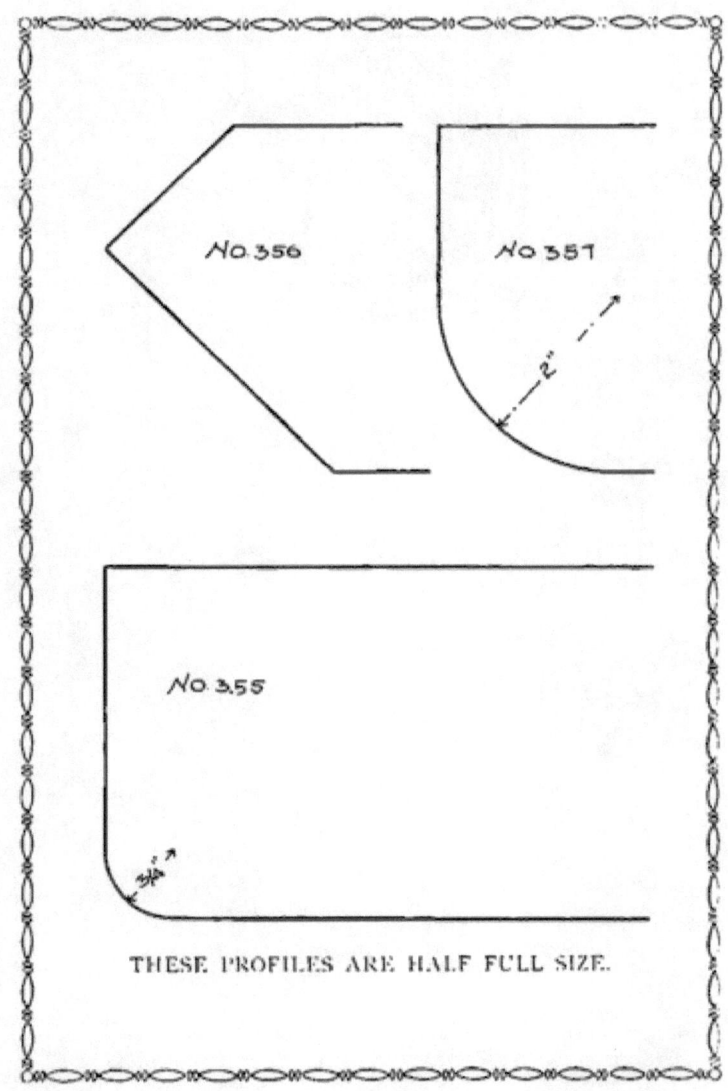

THESE PROFILES ARE HALF FULL SIZE.

SERIES E

PANEL MOULDINGS

BRICKS such as 430 and 431, with their mitre, are suitable for forming panels in walls or in posts where the panels are not on adjacent faces. Bricks such as 430x, which reverses on itself, with its mitre, are suitable for forming panels at the angle of a wall, or in a post, two adjacent sides of which are panelled. Many of the bricks of Series B, D, F, G, and K, may also be used in panels. Suggestions as to ways of doing this will be found on page fifty-nine. Panel mitres are made for any bricks ordered for use in panels.

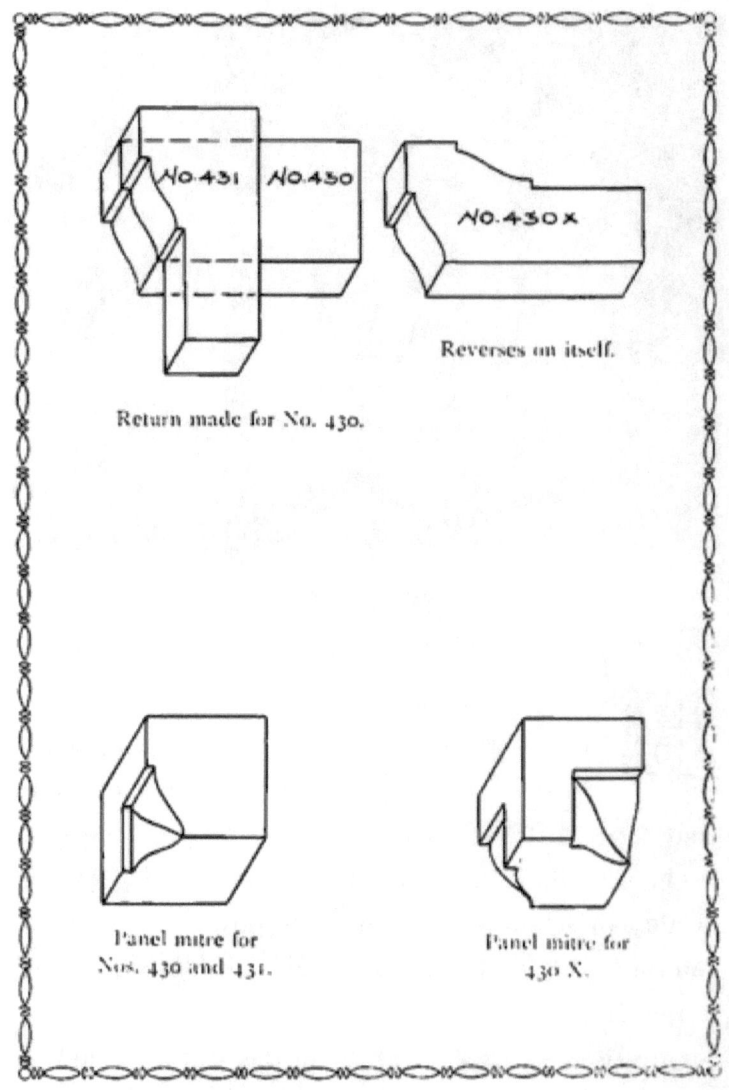

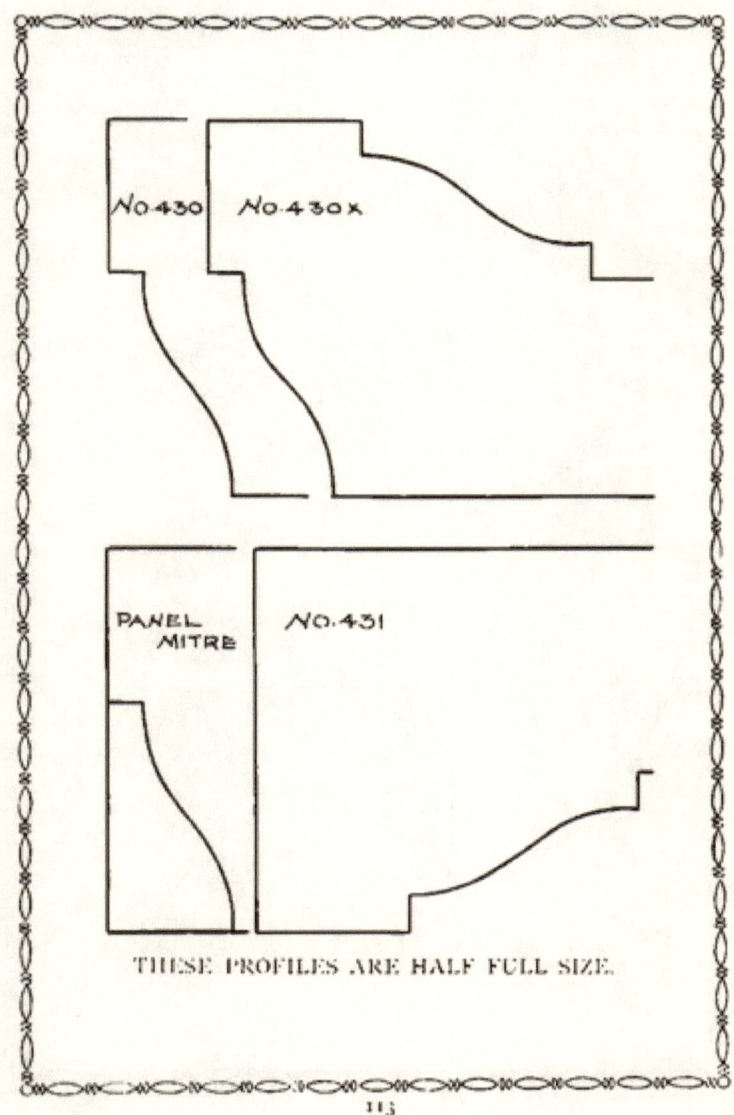

THESE PROFILES ARE HALF FULL SIZE.

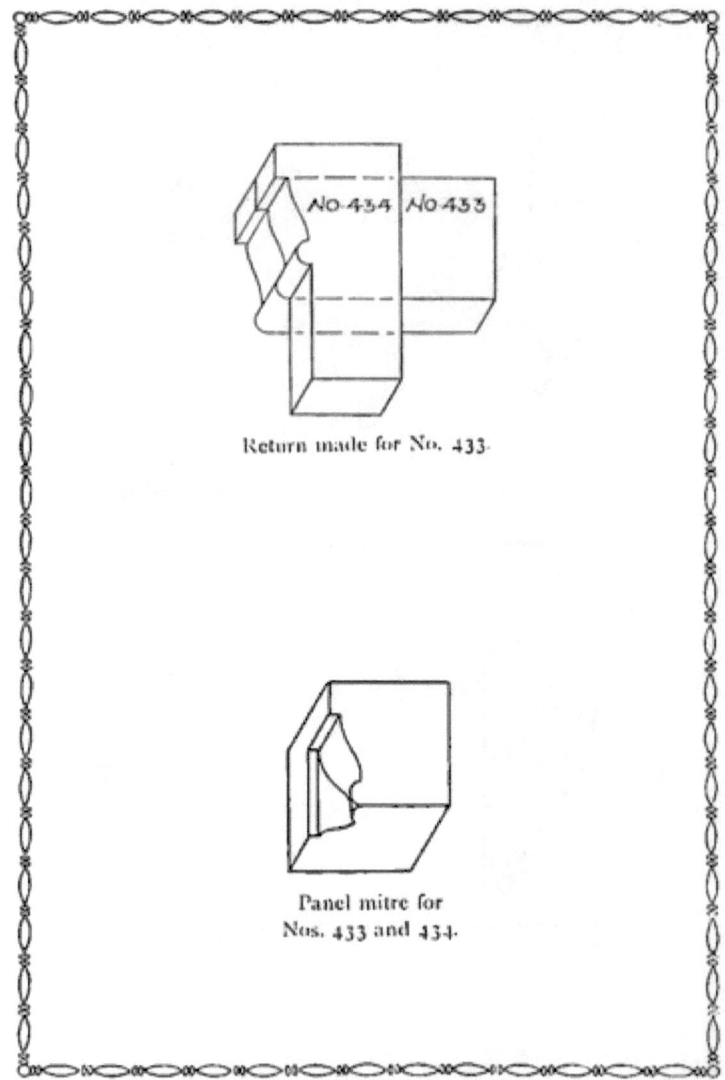

Return made for No. 433.

Panel mitre for
Nos. 433 and 434.

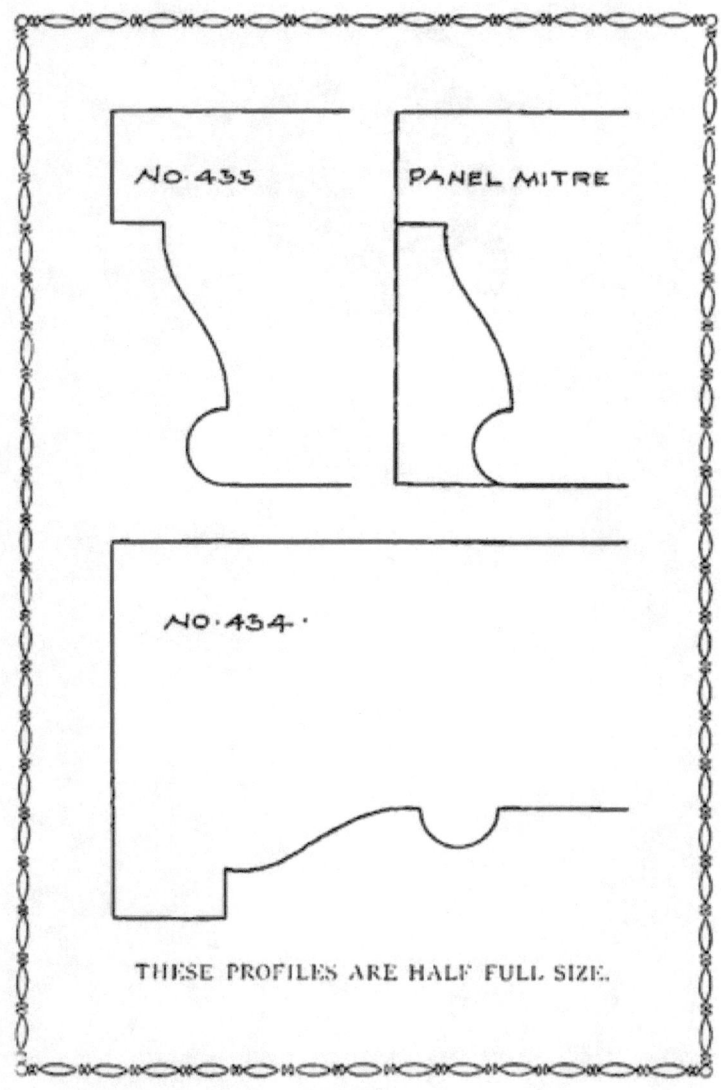

SERIES F

STRING COURSES

THE bricks shown in this section are designed for use in string courses, but nearly all of them are also useful in cornices. Several of them are also useful for other purposes, *e.g.*, the checker bricks, for enriching flat surfaces, as shown around the arches at the top of this page. Other bricks suitable for use as string courses may be found in Series B, D, G, H, and K.

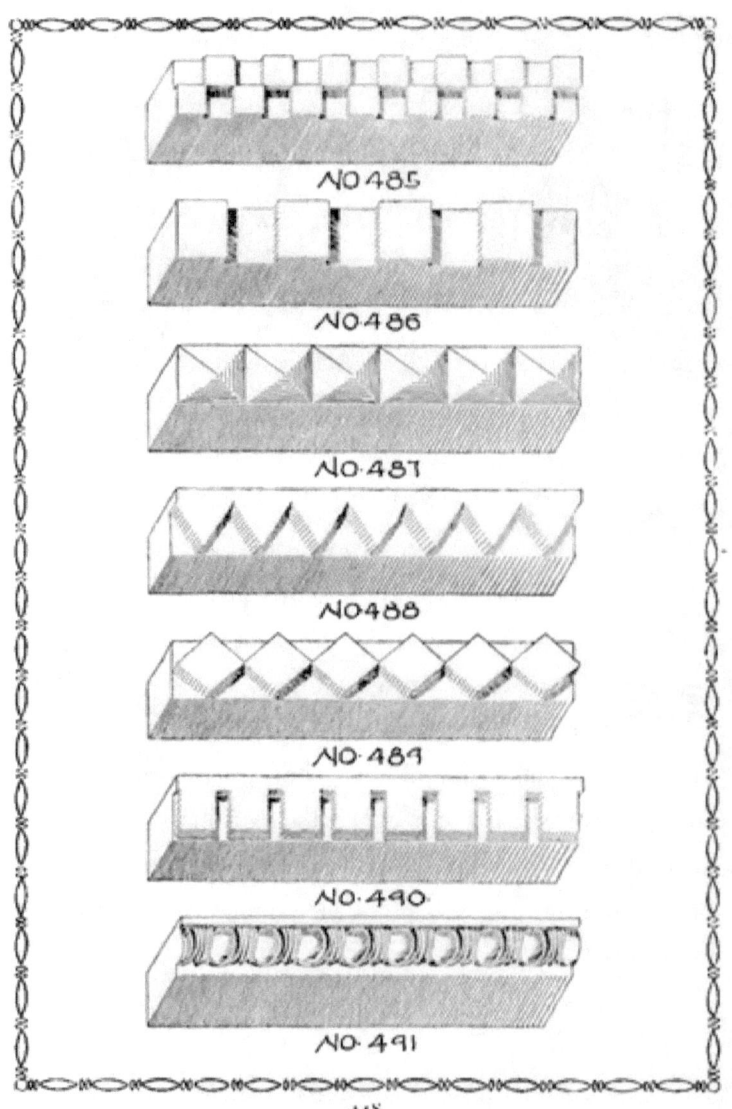

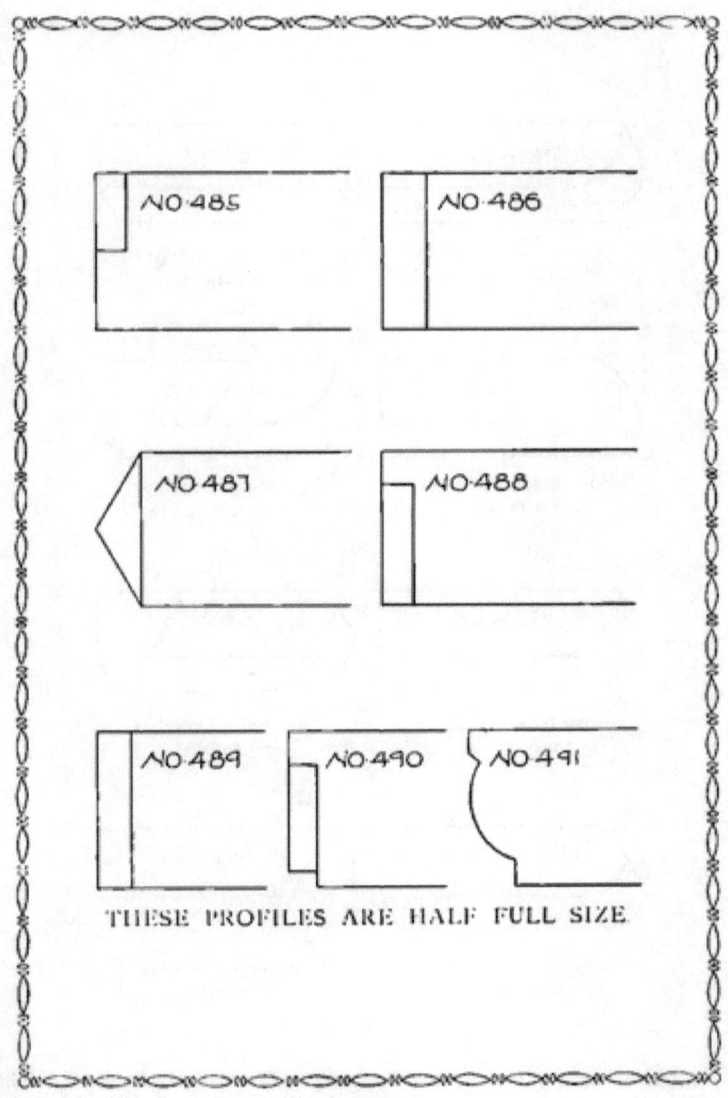

THESE PROFILES ARE HALF FULL SIZE.

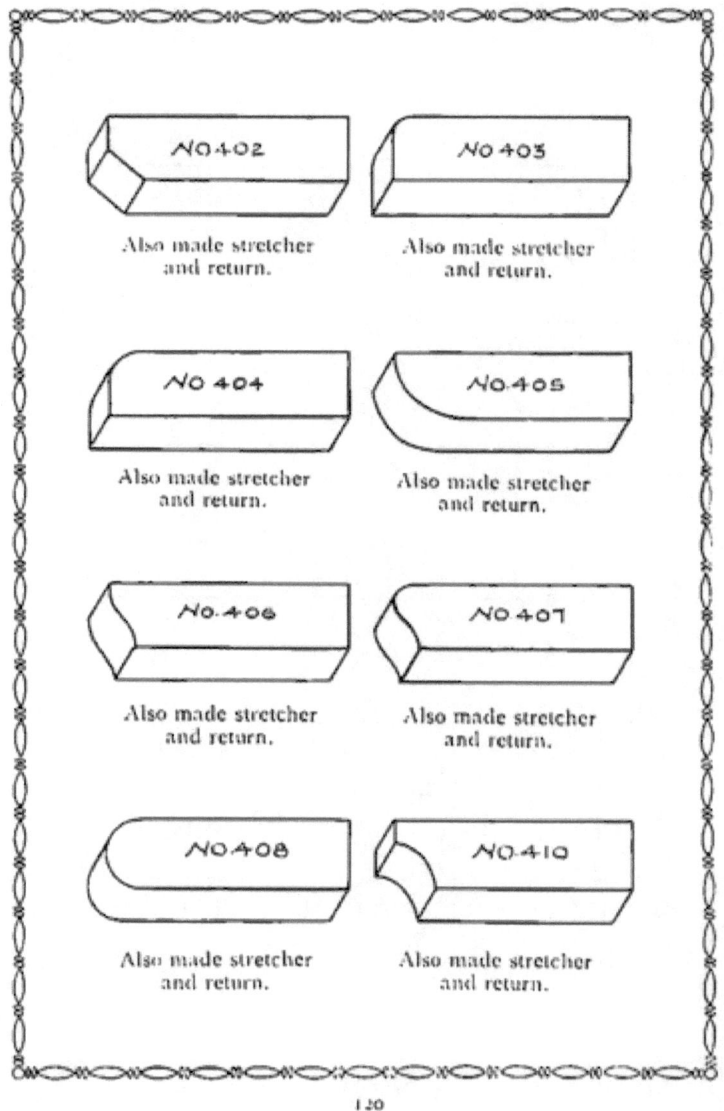

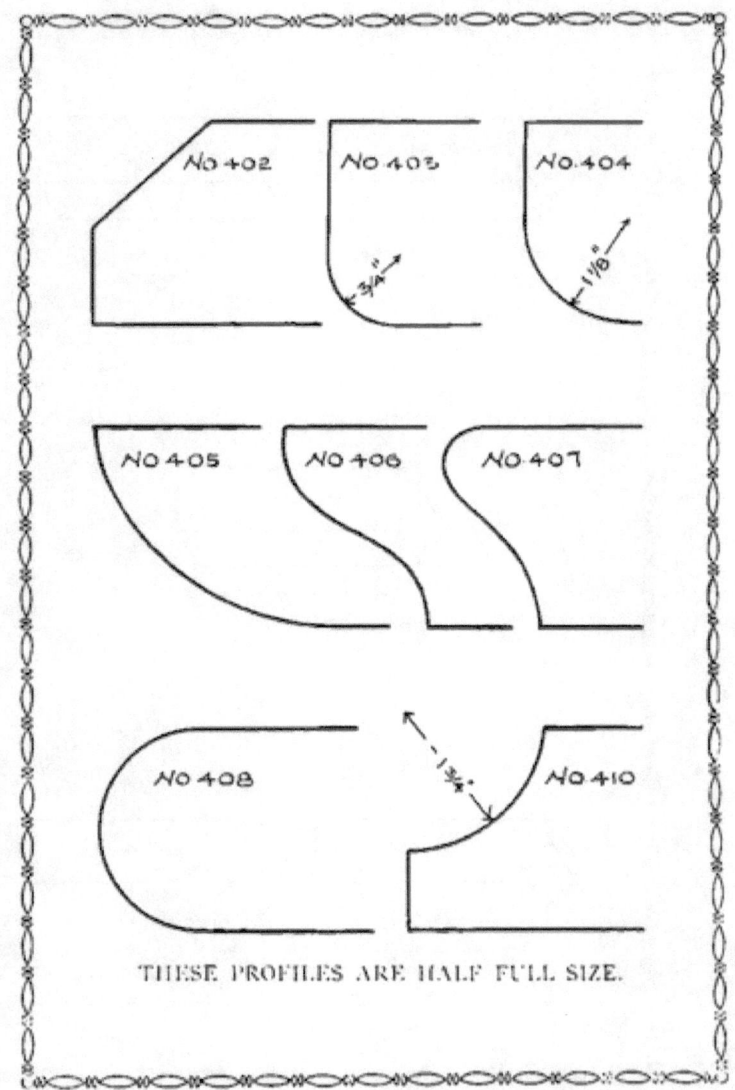

THESE PROFILES ARE HALF FULL SIZE.

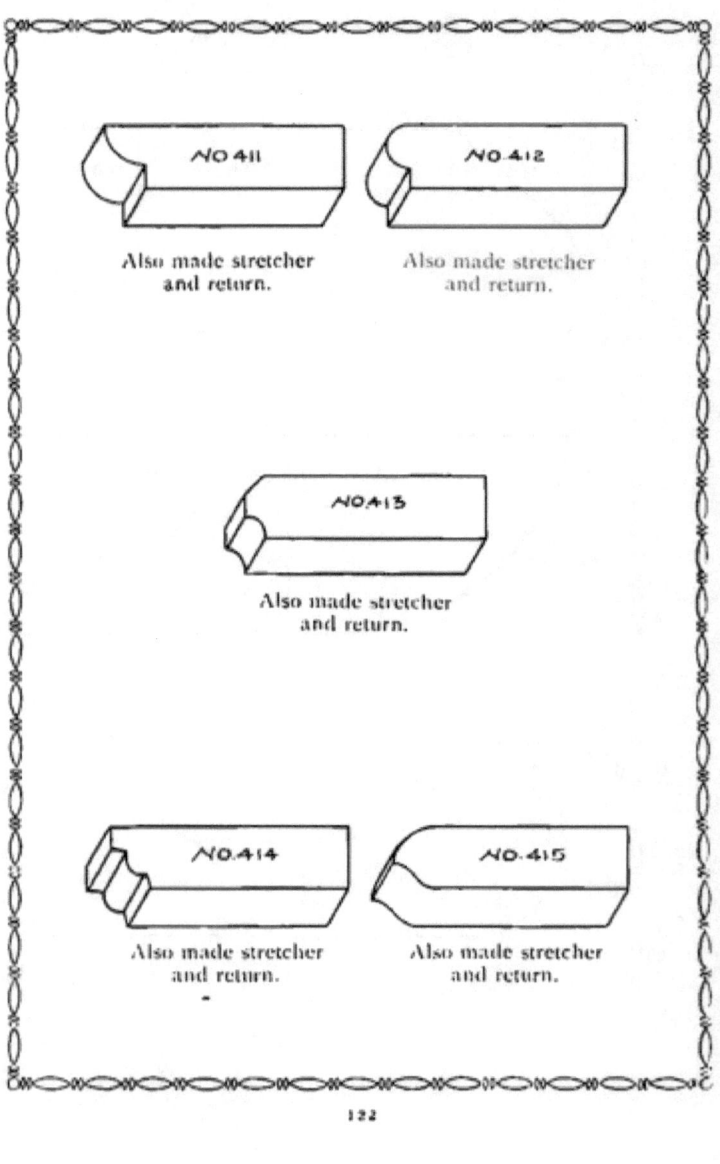

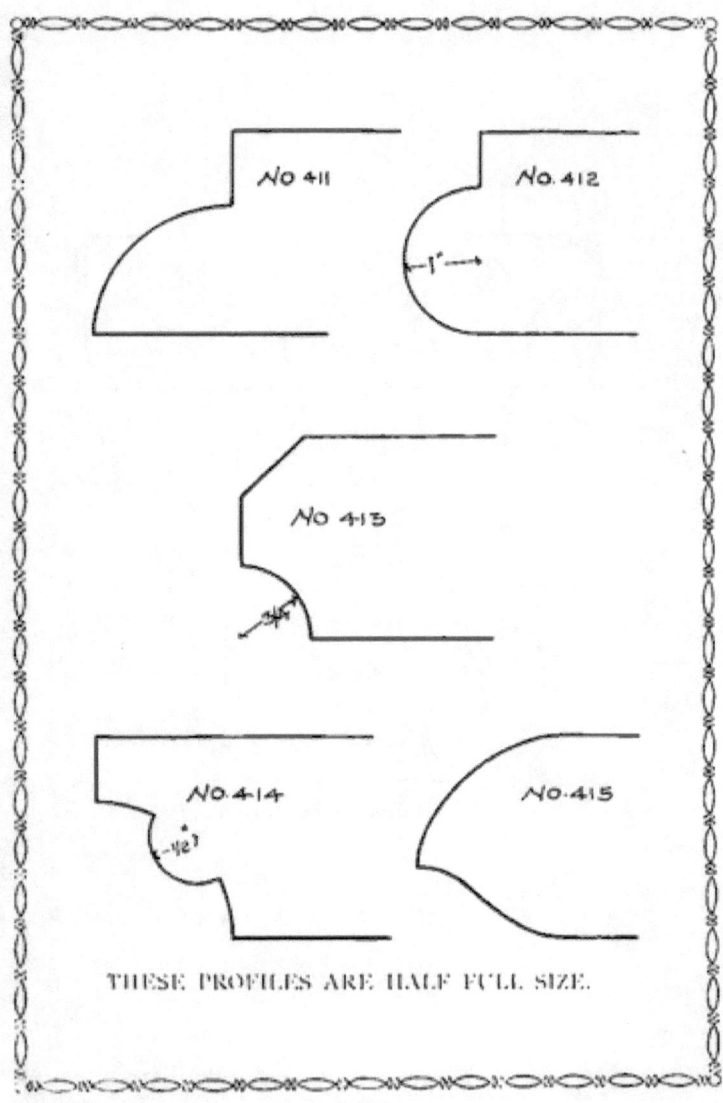

THESE PROFILES ARE HALF FULL SIZE.

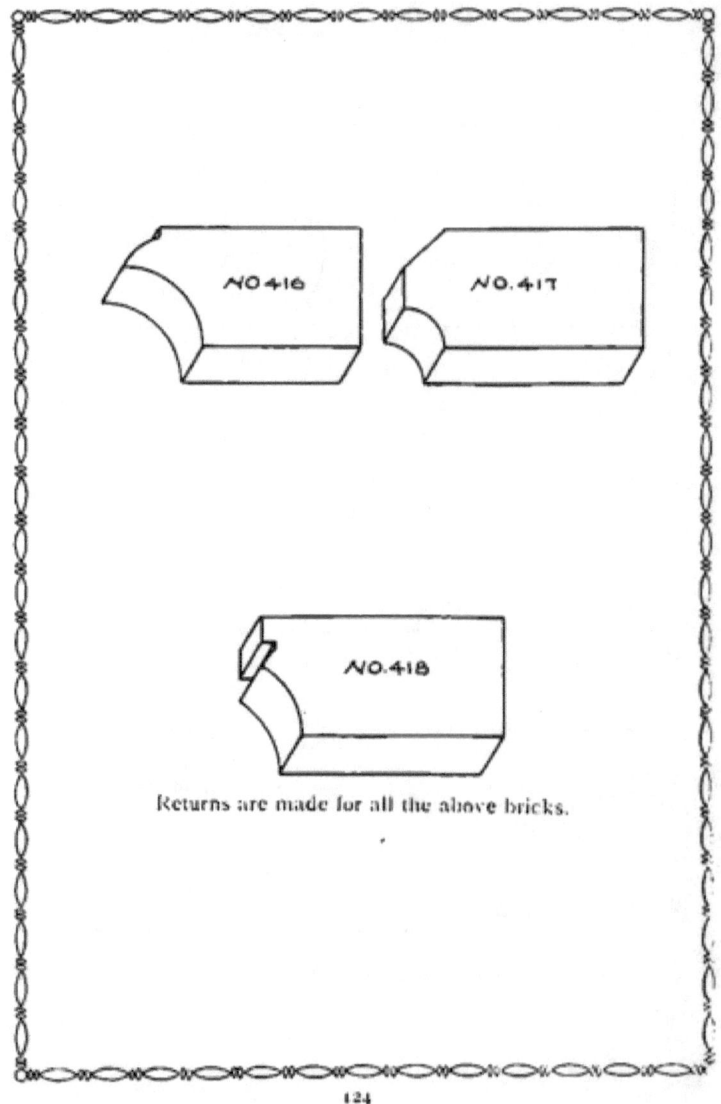

Returns are made for all the above bricks.

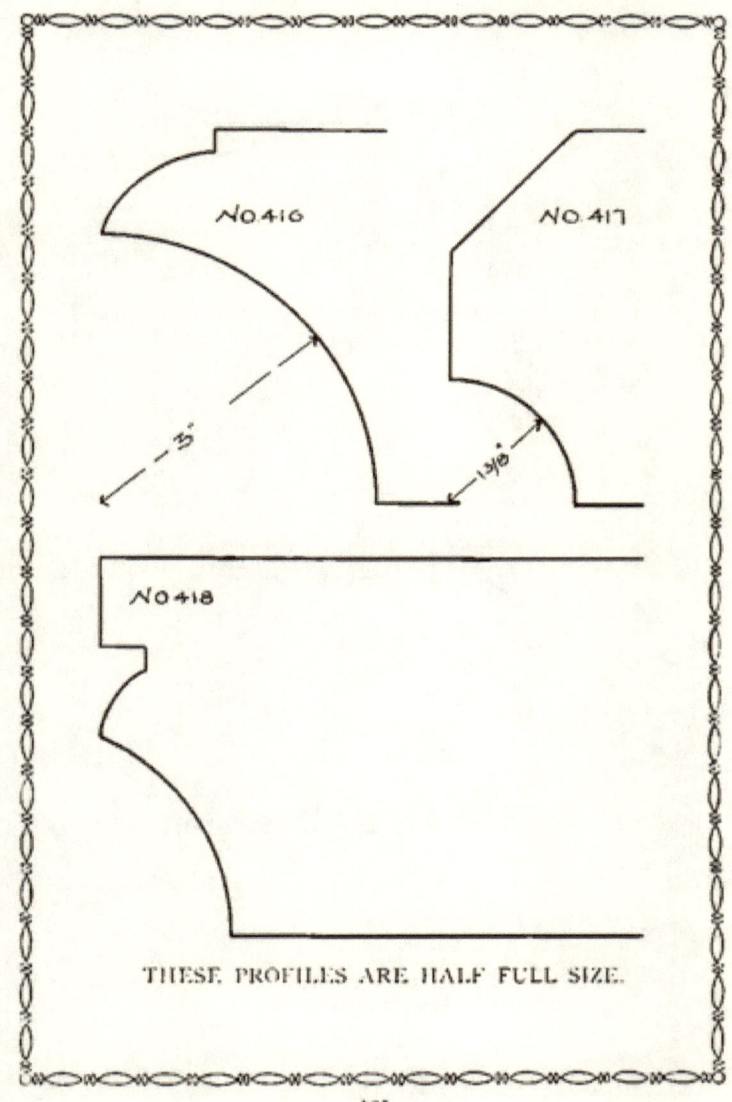

THESE PROFILES ARE HALF FULL SIZE.

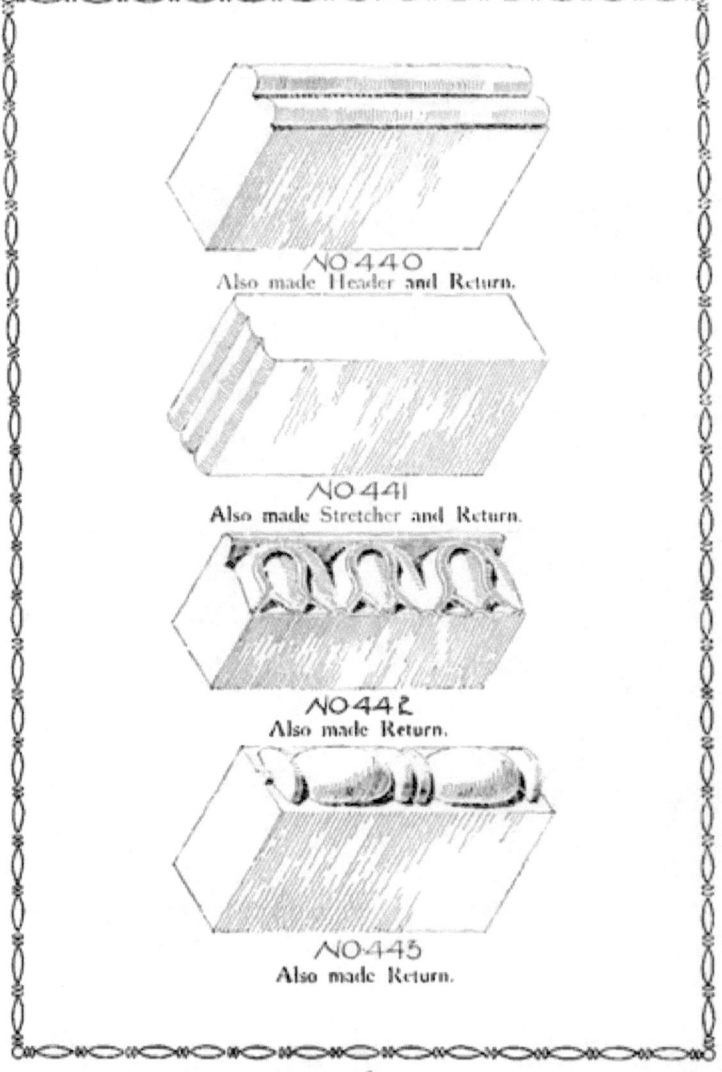

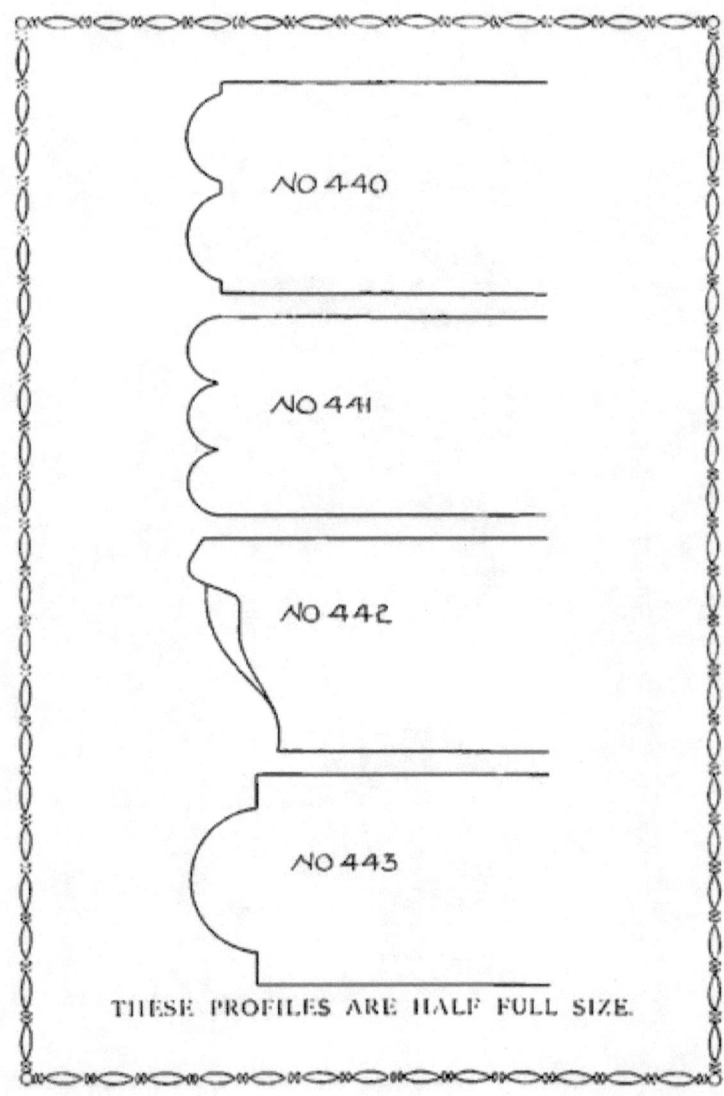

THESE PROFILES ARE HALF FULL SIZE.

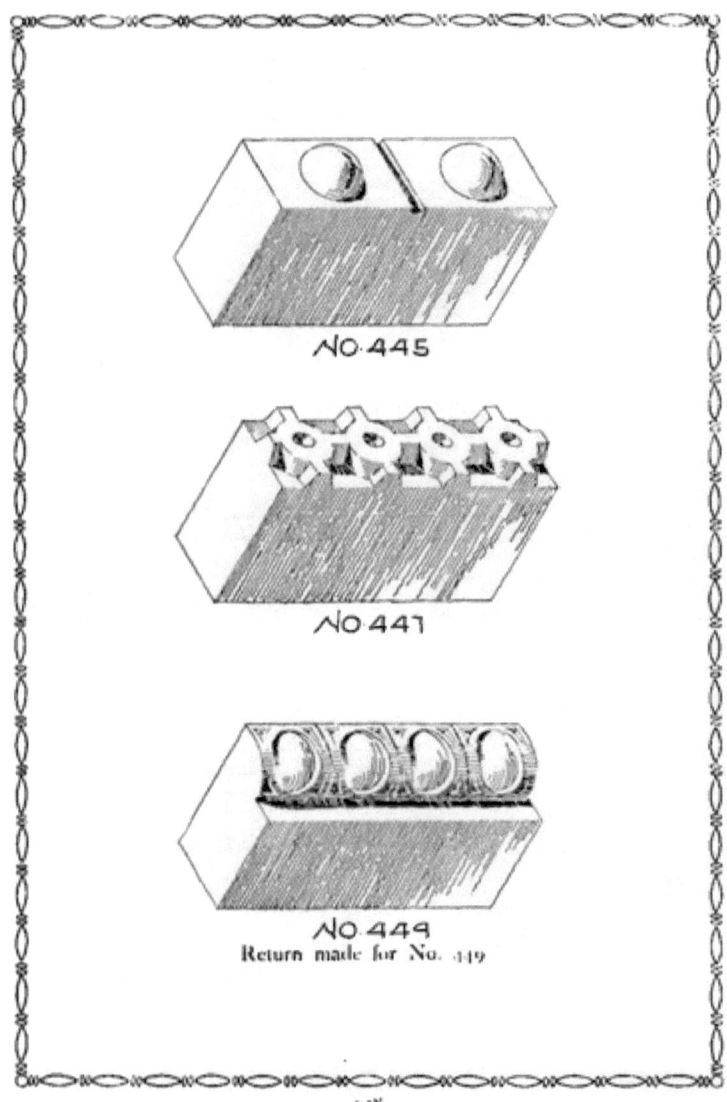

No. 445

No. 447

No. 449
Return made for No. 449

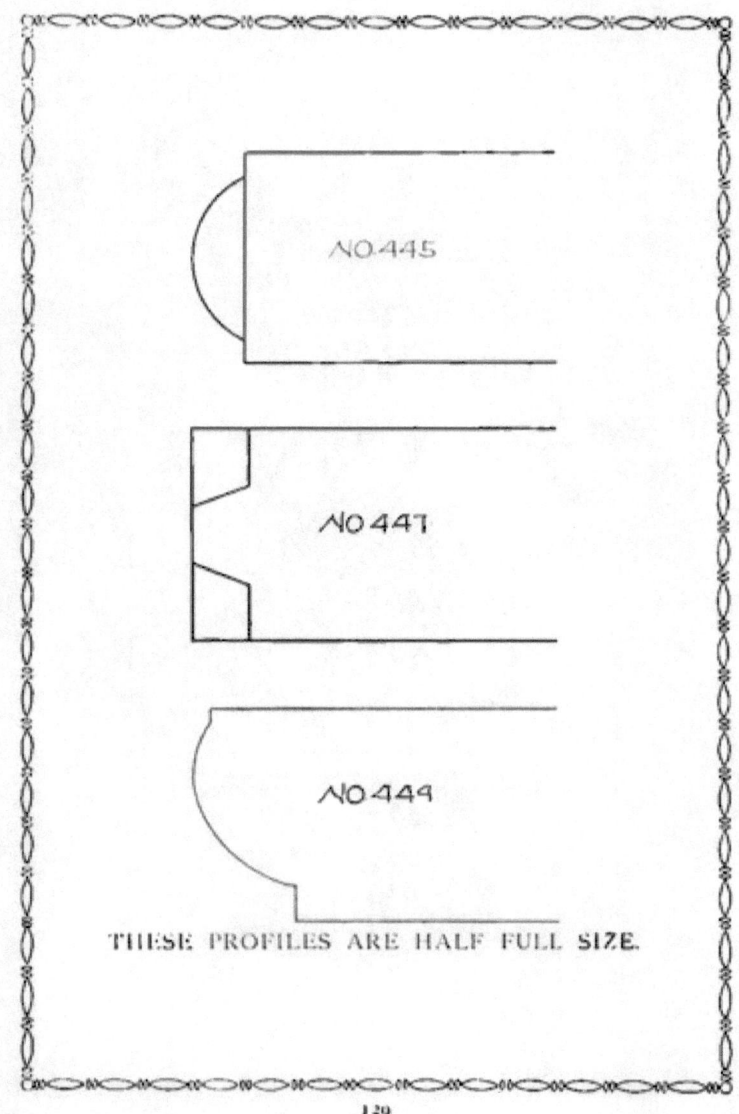

THESE PROFILES ARE HALF FULL SIZE.

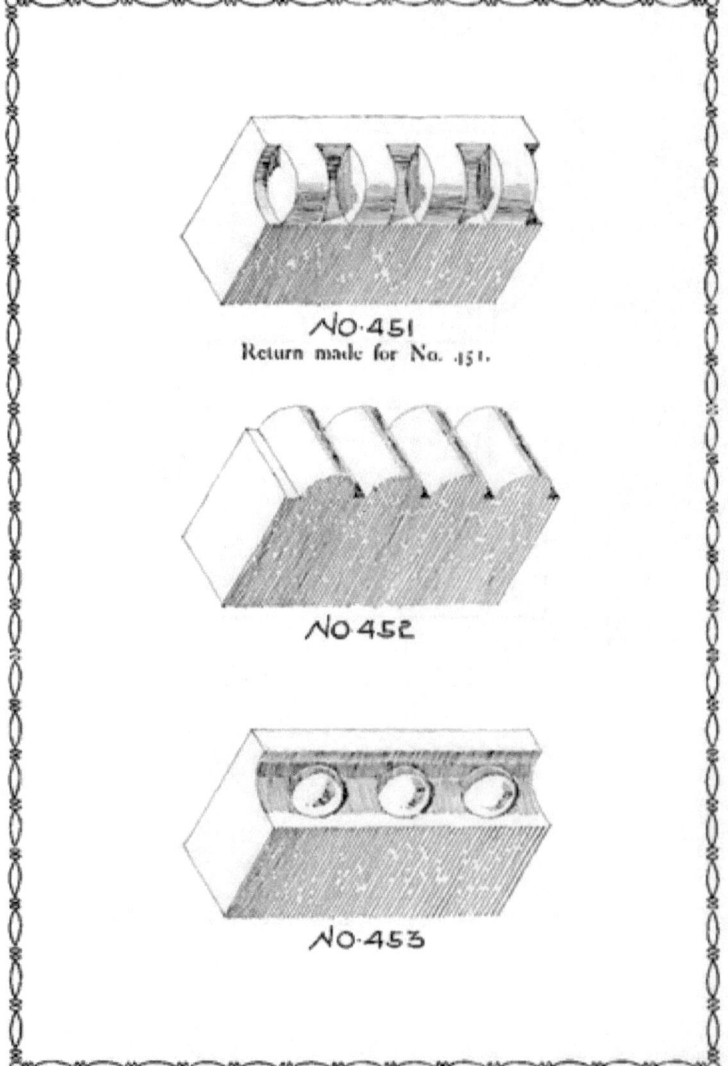

No. 451
Return made for No. 451.

No. 452

No. 453

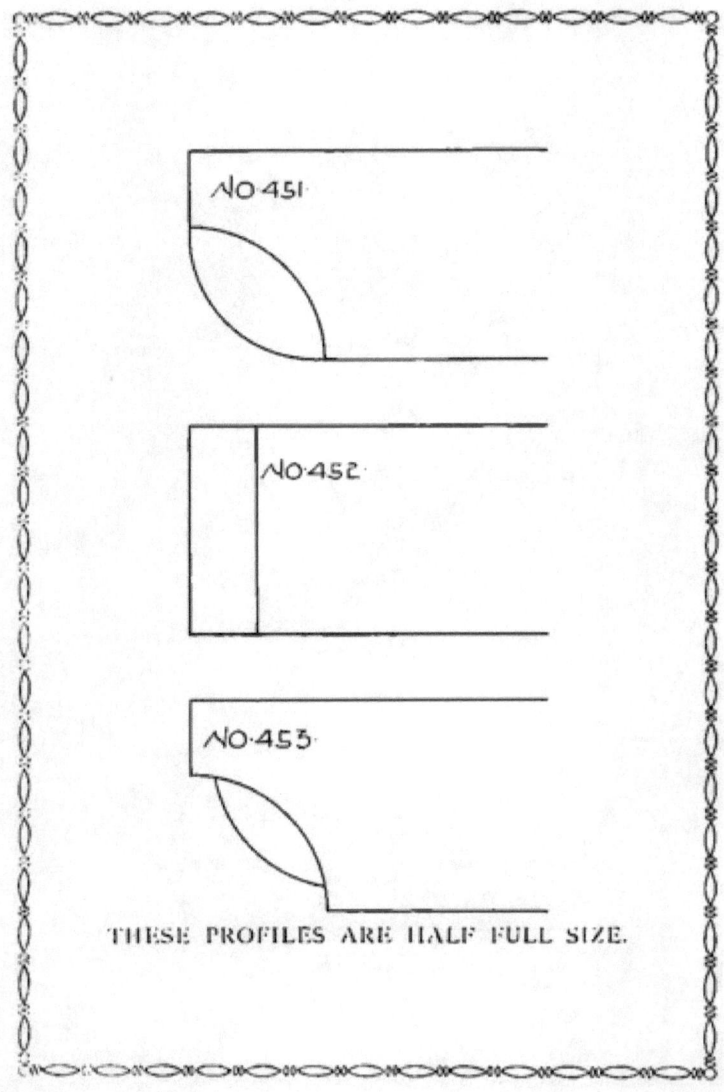

THESE PROFILES ARE HALF FULL SIZE.

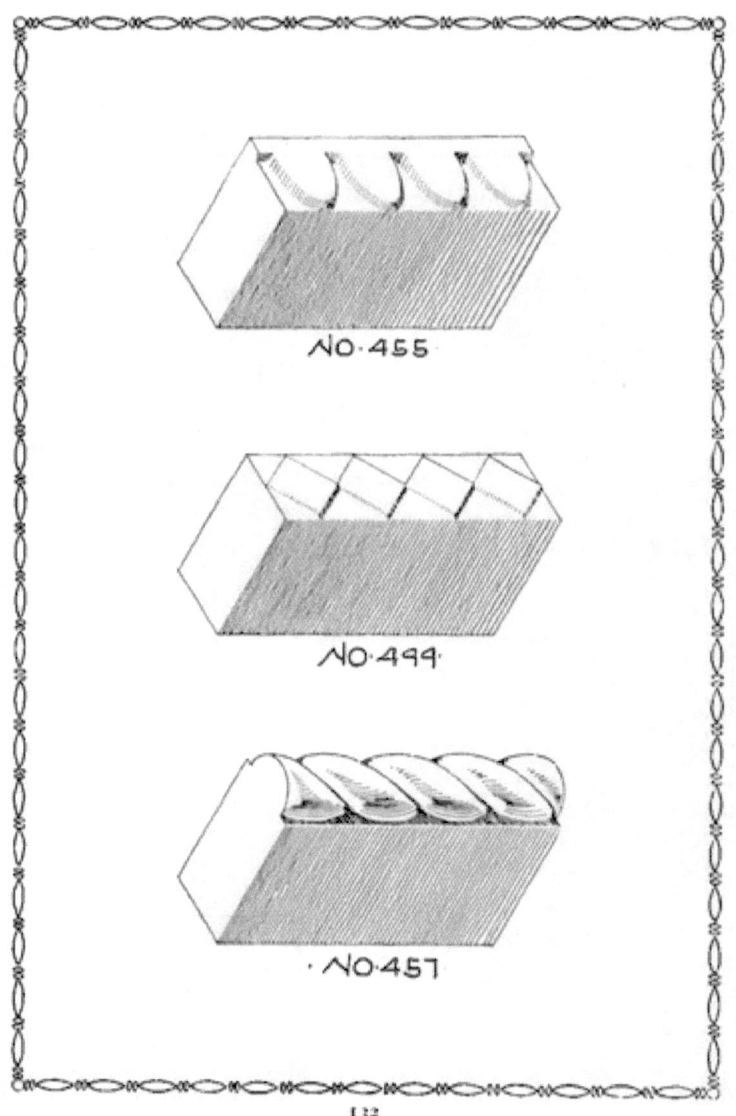

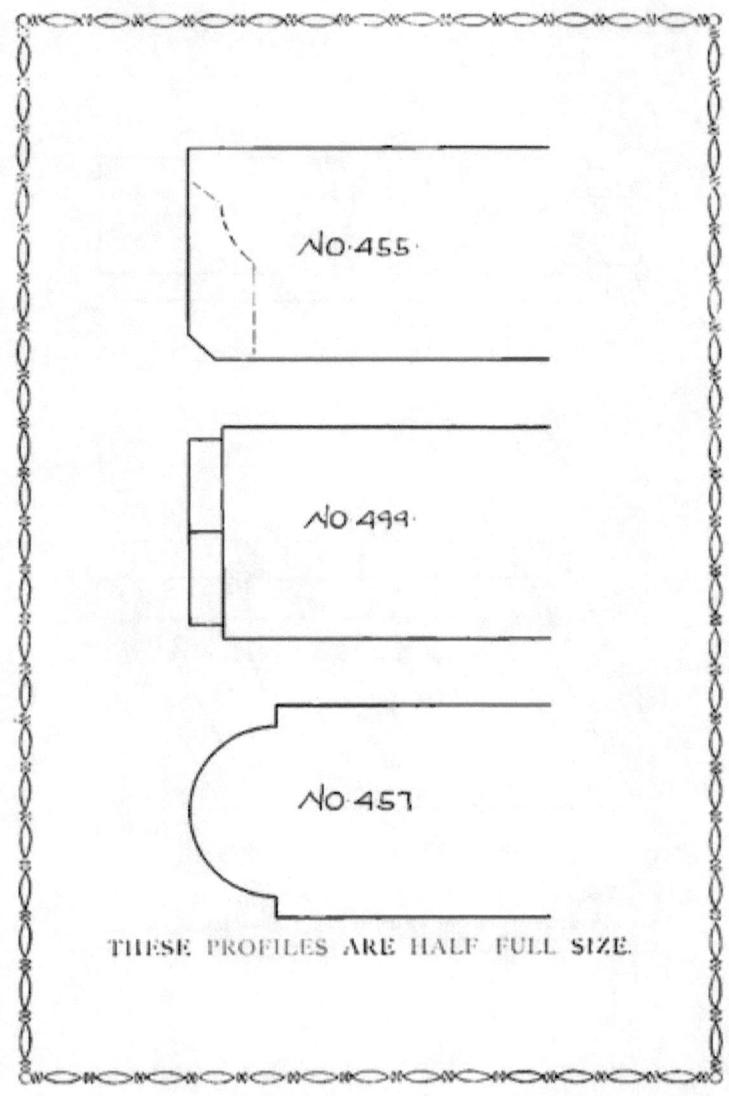

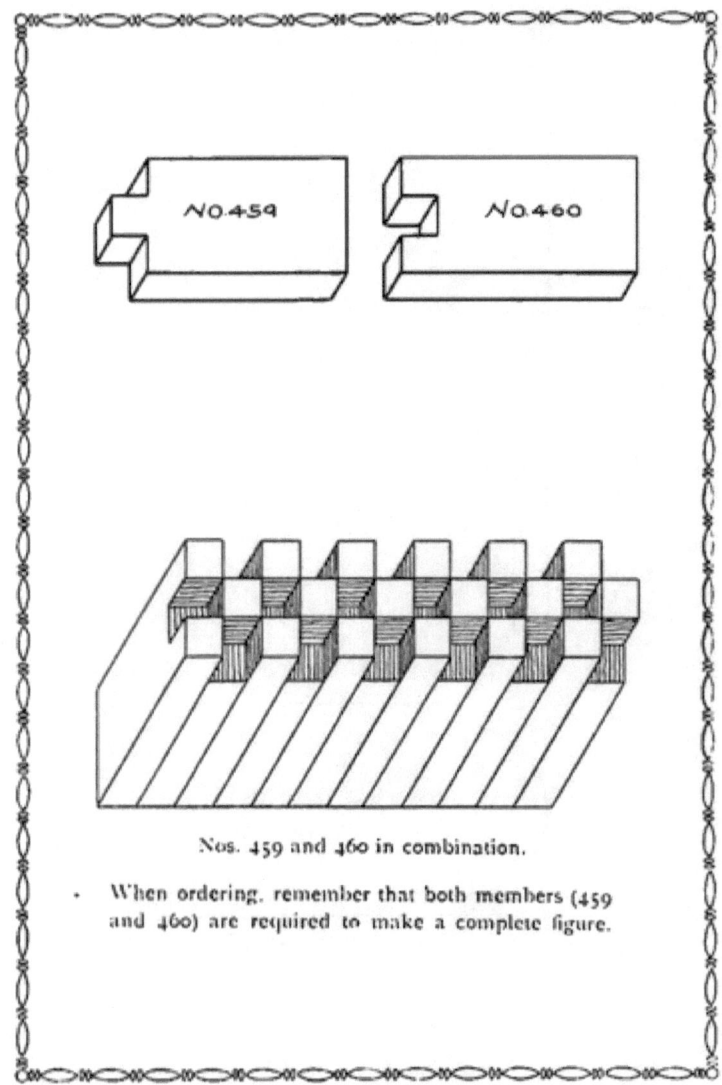

Nos. 459 and 460 in combination.

When ordering, remember that both members (459 and 460) are required to make a complete figure.

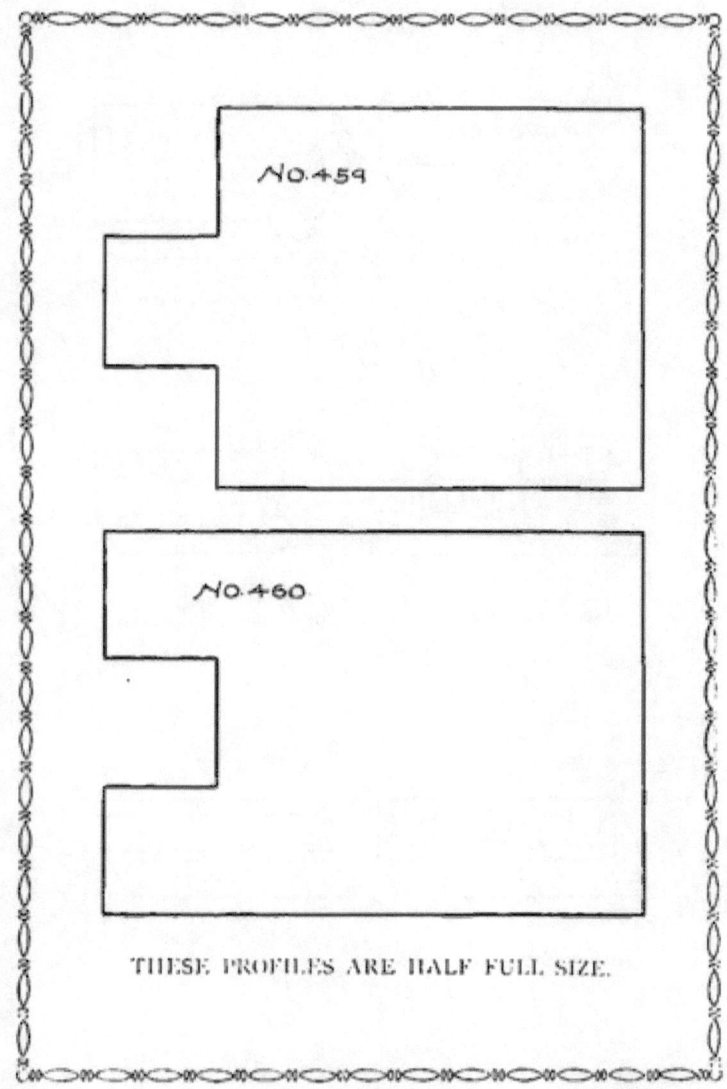

THESE PROFILES ARE HALF FULL SIZE.

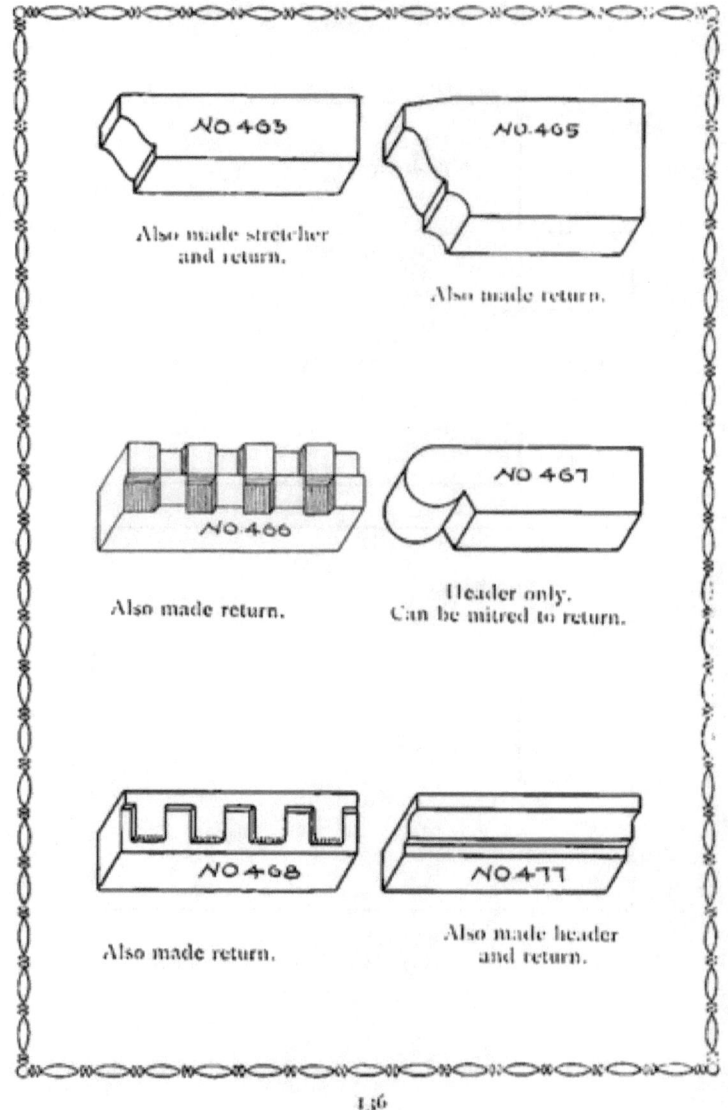

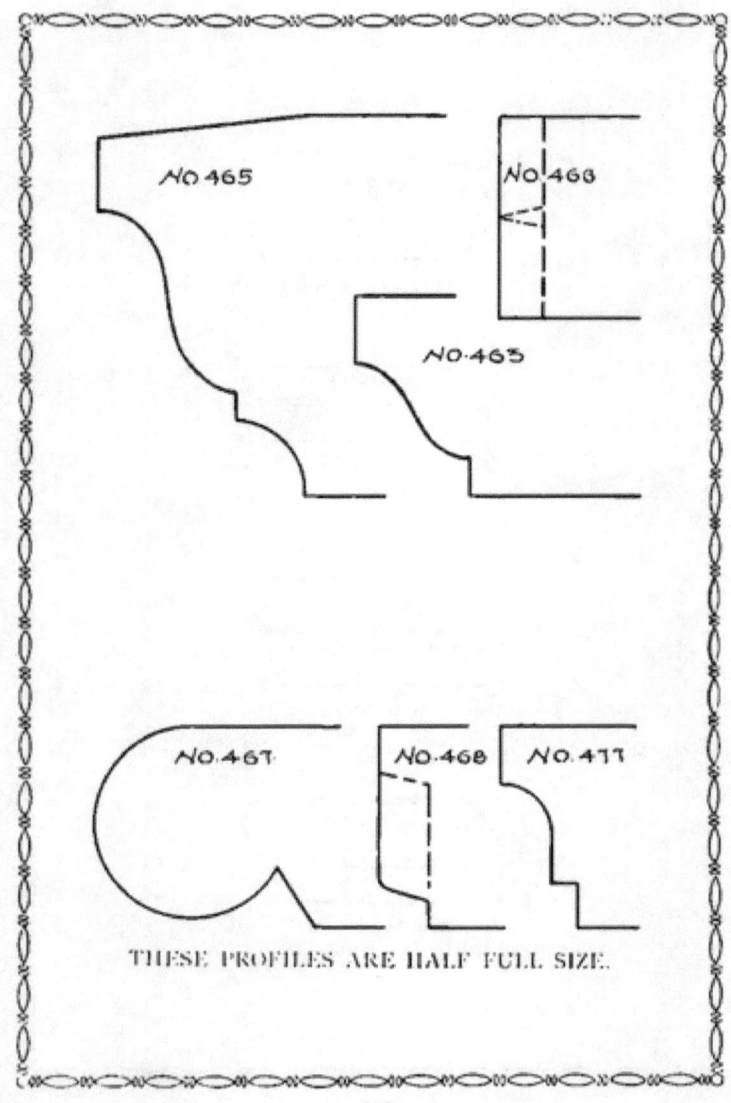

THESE PROFILES ARE HALF FULL SIZE.

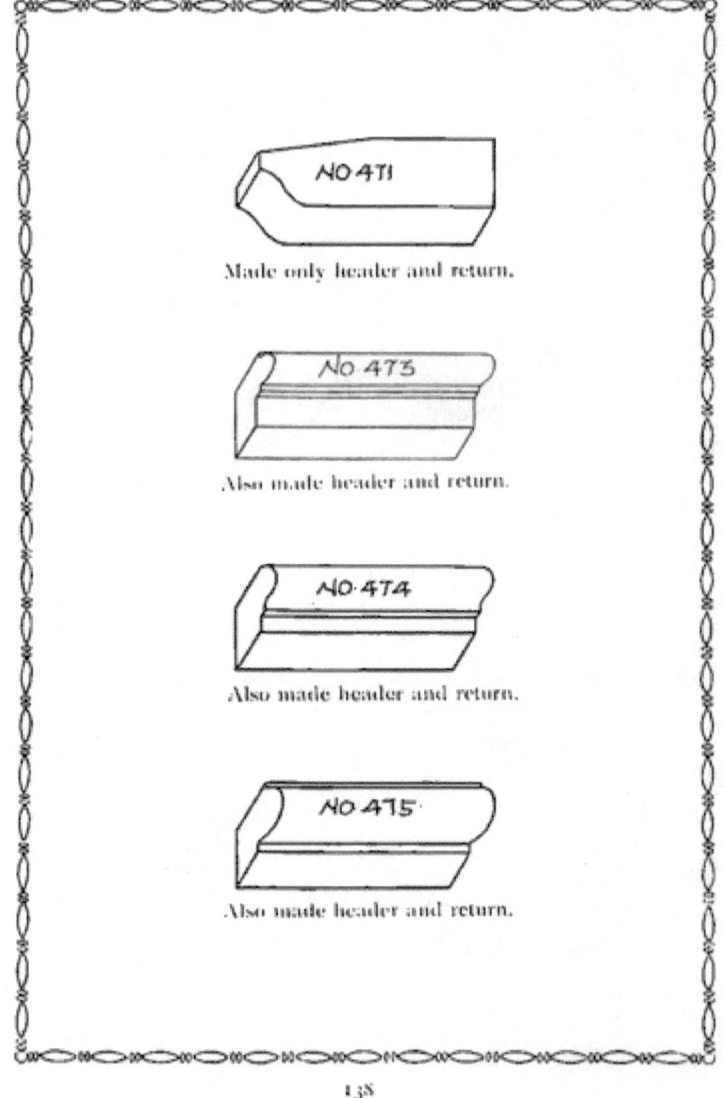

No. 471
Made only header and return.

No. 473
Also made header and return.

No. 474
Also made header and return.

No. 475
Also made header and return.

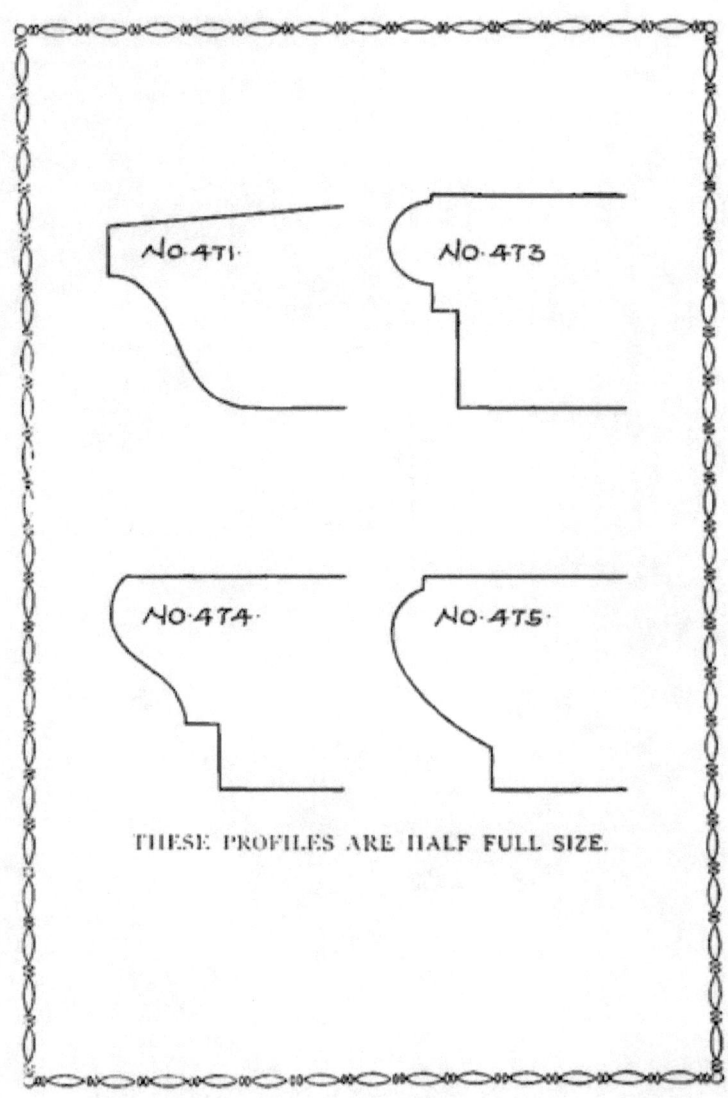

THESE PROFILES ARE HALF FULL SIZE.

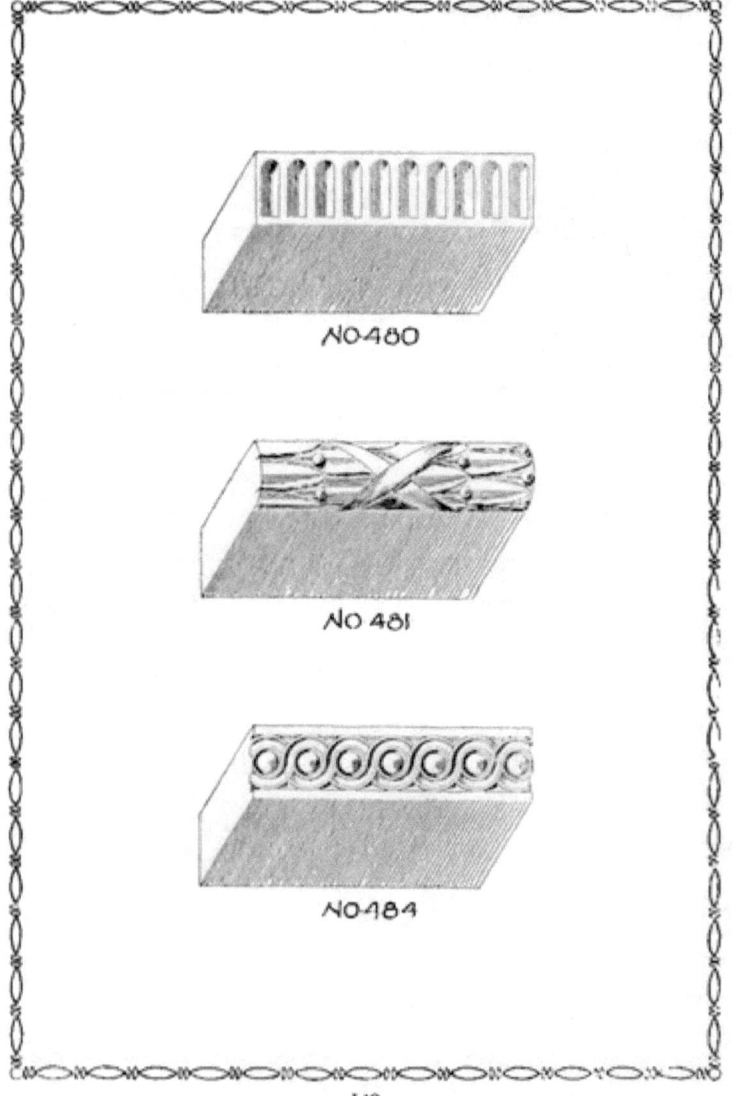

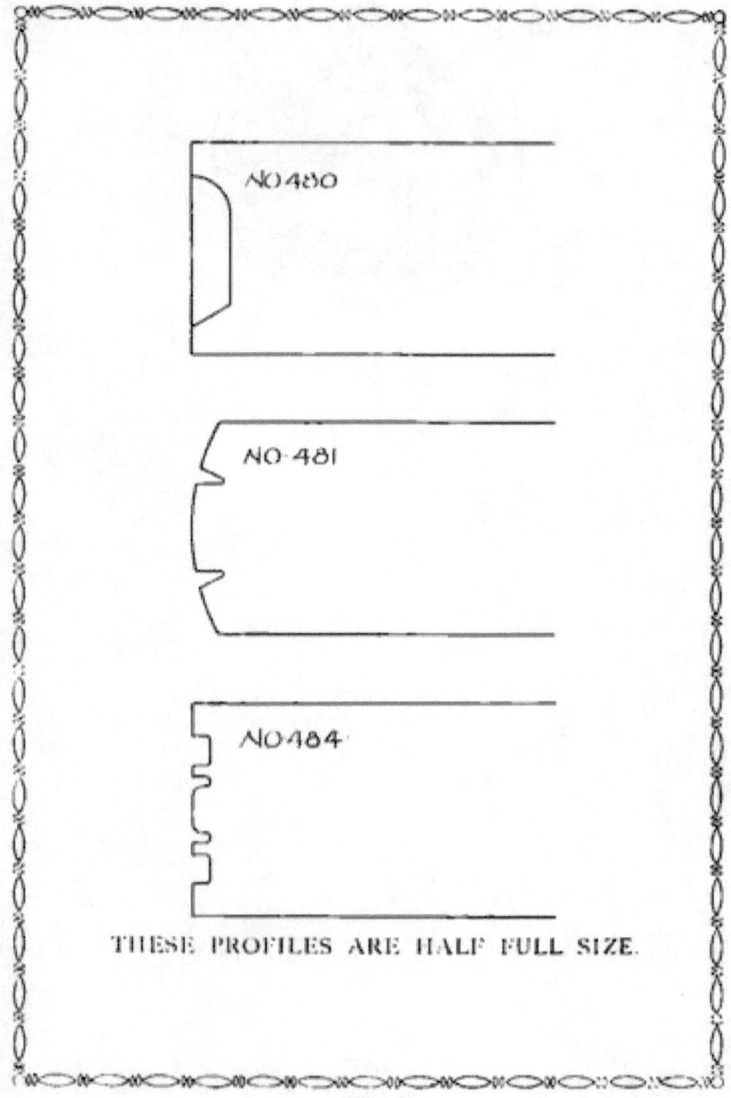

THESE PROFILES ARE HALF FULL SIZE.

SERIES G

CORNICE MOULDINGS

THE bricks shown in this section have been designed for use in cornices, and their effect when so used may be seen in the cornices, pages twenty-eight to thirty-three. Many of them may also be used as jambs or in string courses. Additional bricks suitable for use in cornices may be found in Sections B, D, E, F, and K.

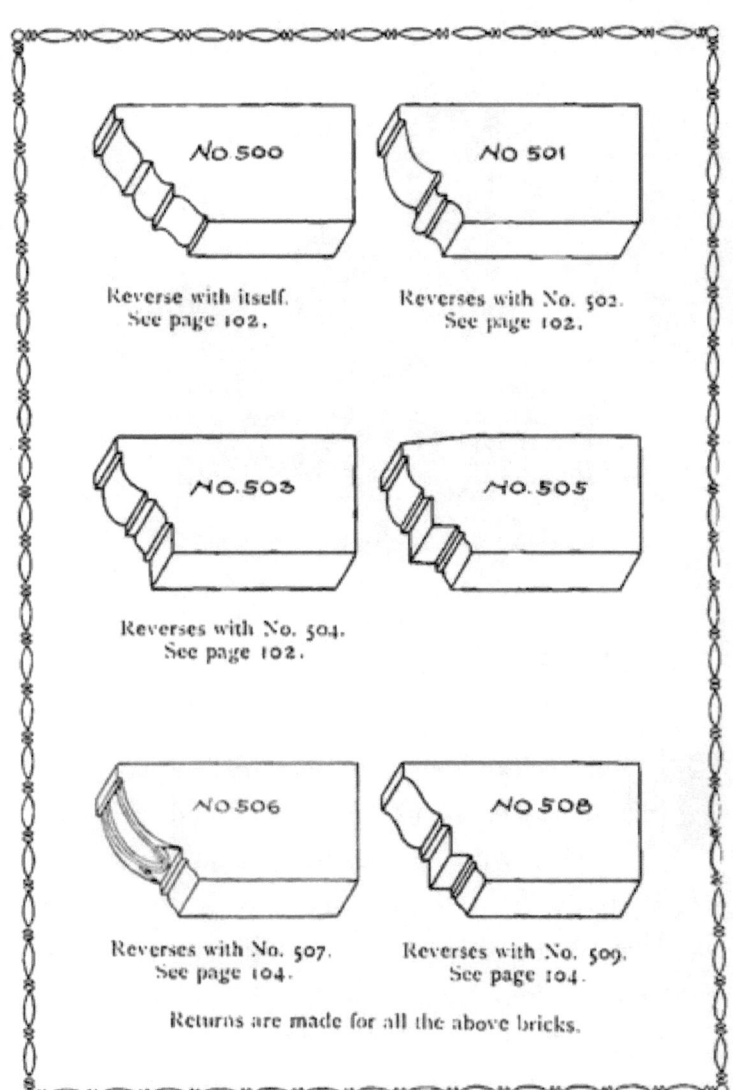

No 500 — Reverse with itself. See page 102.

No 501 — Reverses with No. 502. See page 102.

No. 503 — Reverses with No. 504. See page 102.

No. 505

No 506 — Reverses with No. 507. See page 104.

No 508 — Reverses with No. 509. See page 104.

Returns are made for all the above bricks.

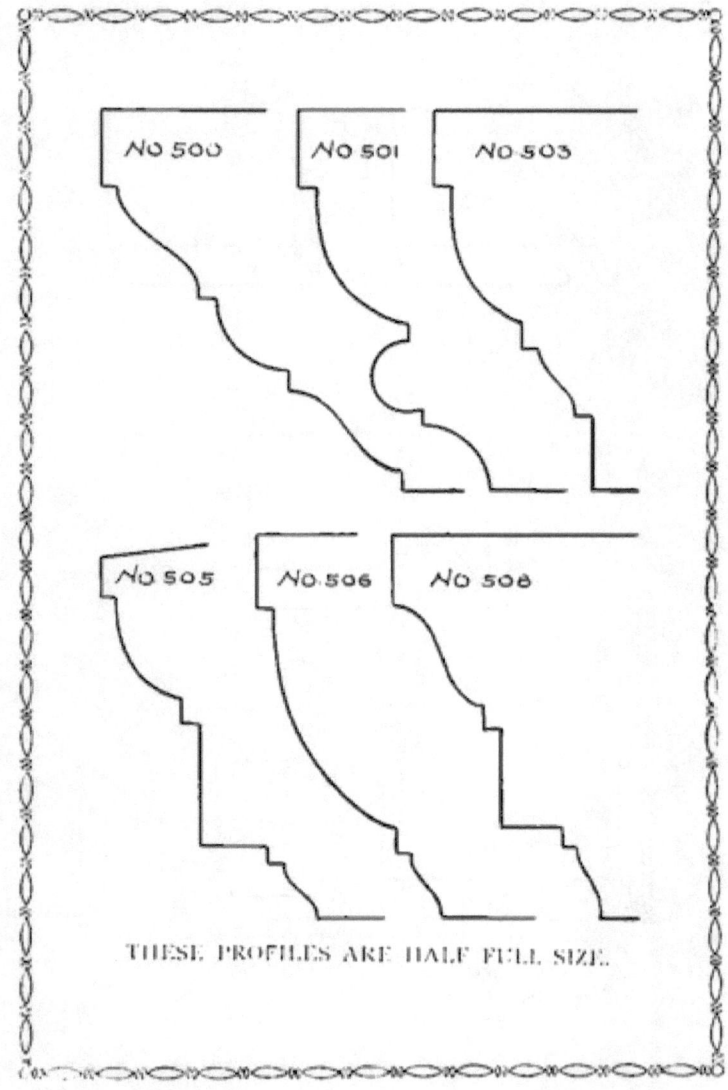

THESE PROFILES ARE HALF FULL SIZE.

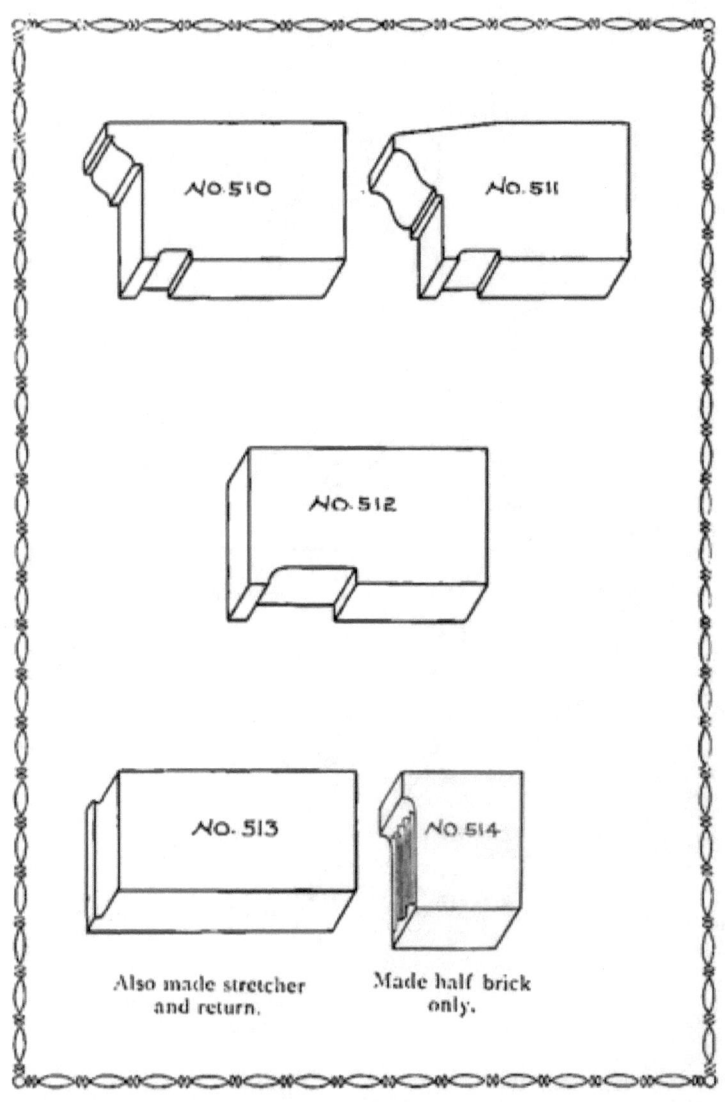

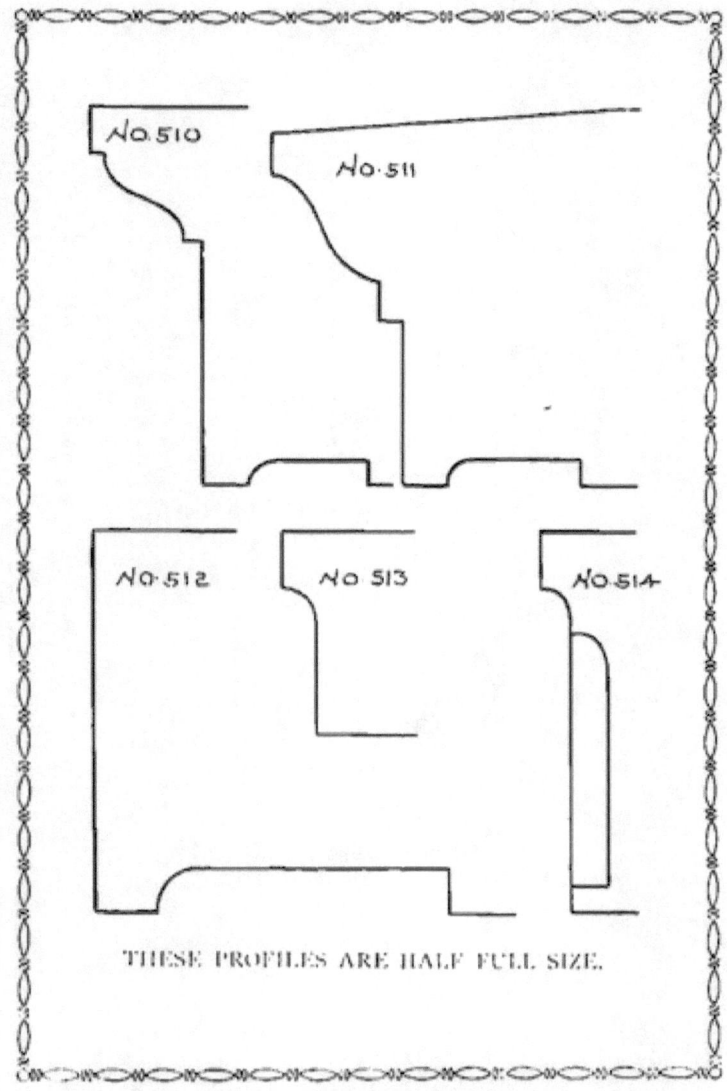

THESE PROFILES ARE HALF FULL SIZE.

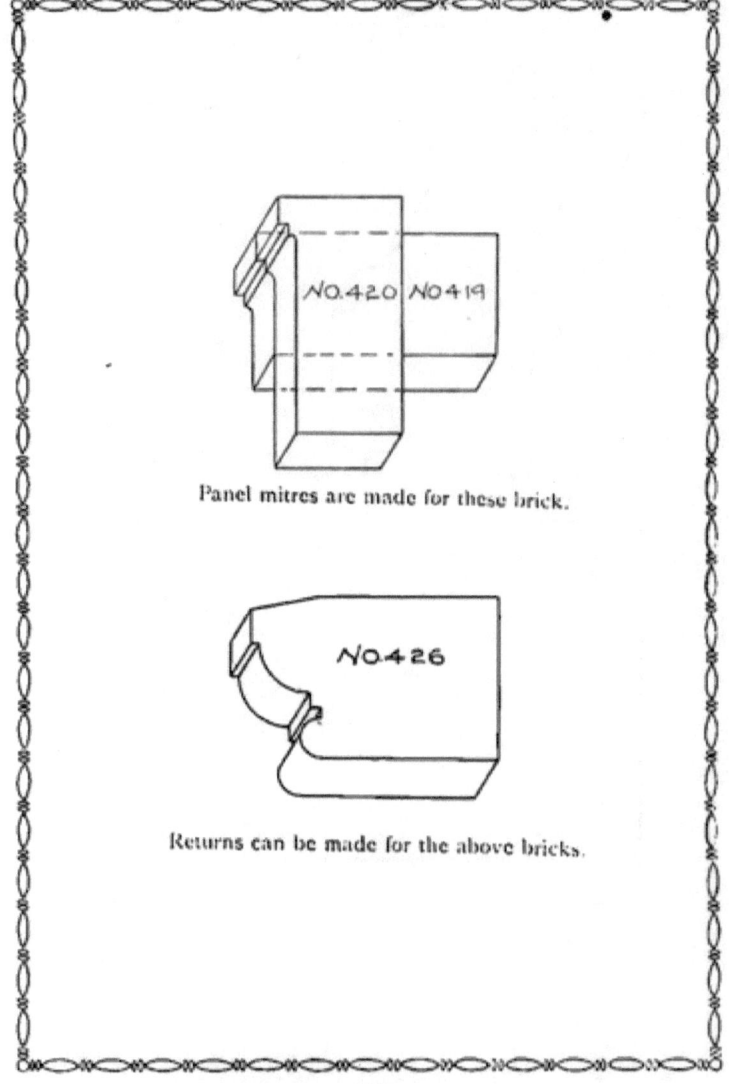

Panel mitres are made for these brick.

Returns can be made for the above bricks.

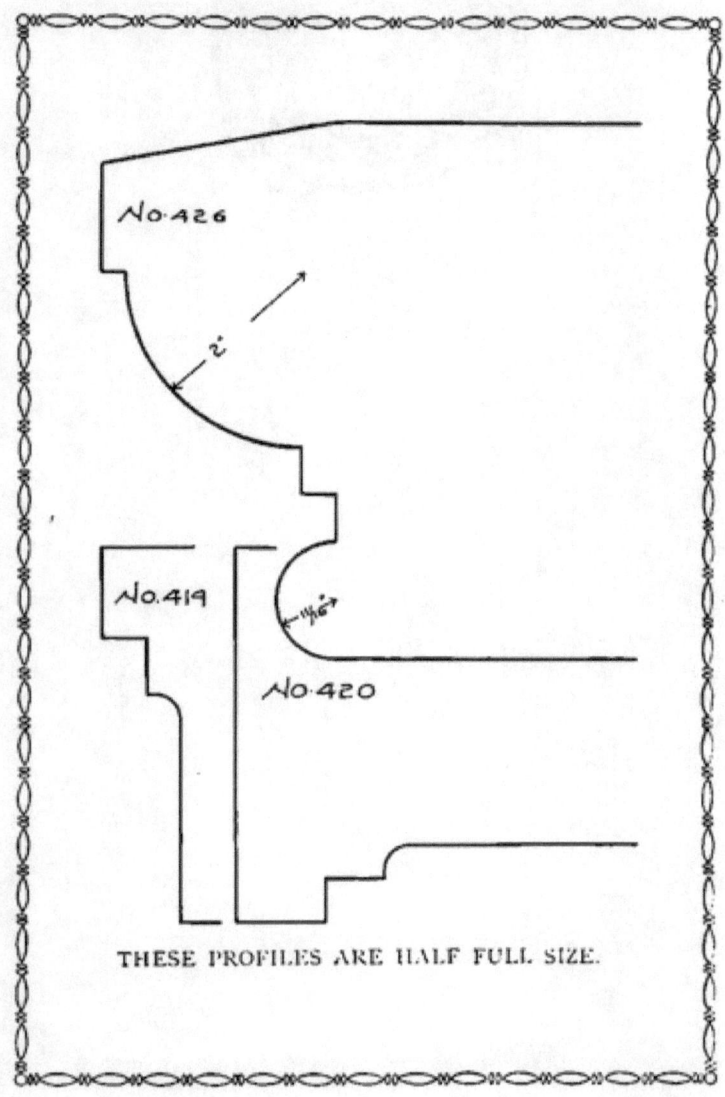

THESE PROFILES ARE HALF FULL SIZE.

SERIES H

BASE MOULDINGS

THE bricks shown in this section are especially suitable for bases. Their effect in combination will be seen on page one hundred and fifty-four. Other bricks suitable for use as base mouldings will be found in Series B, D, E, F, G, and K.

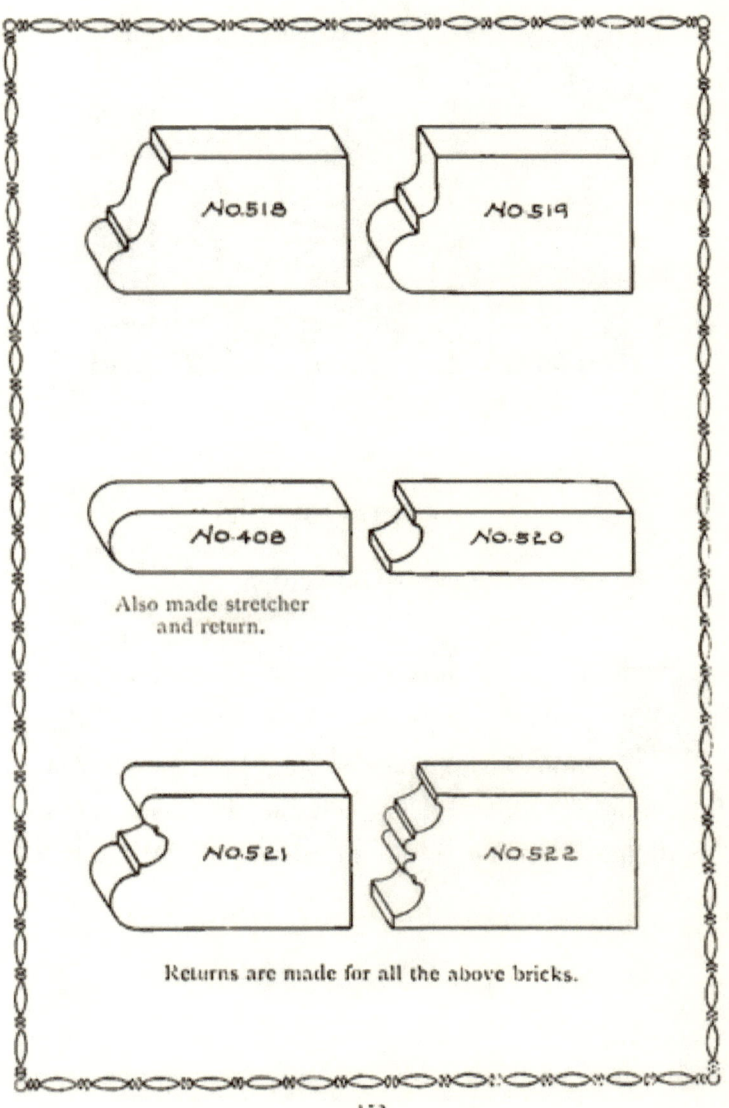

Also made stretcher
and return.

Returns are made for all the above bricks.

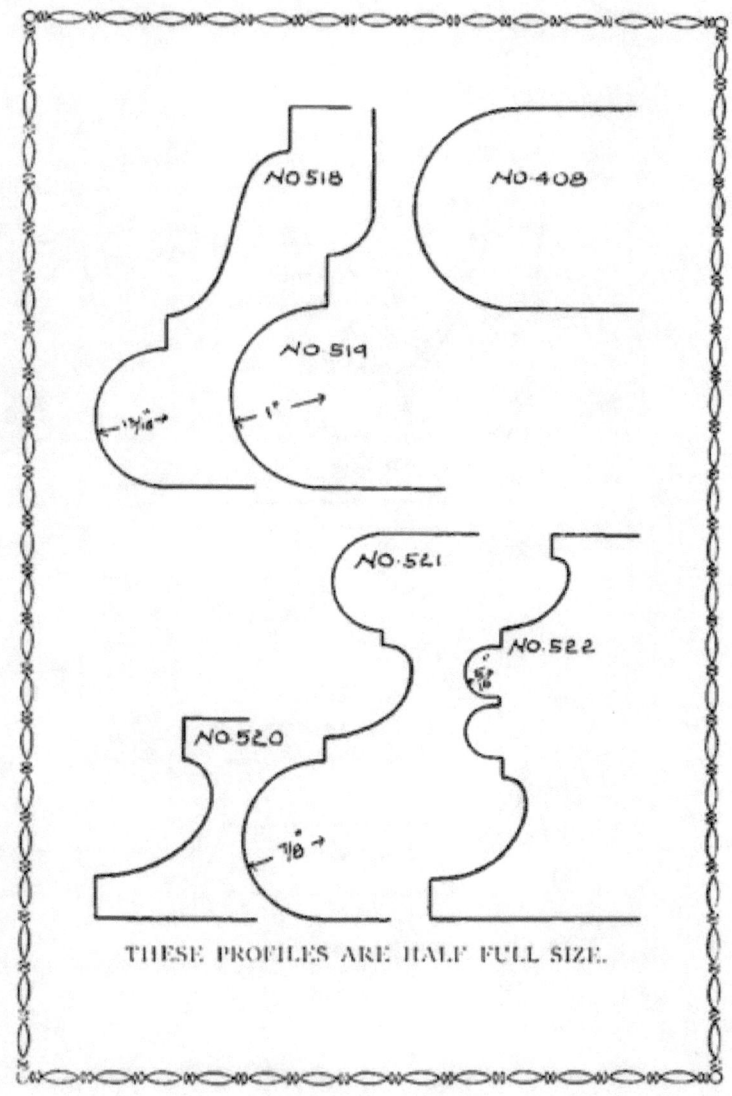

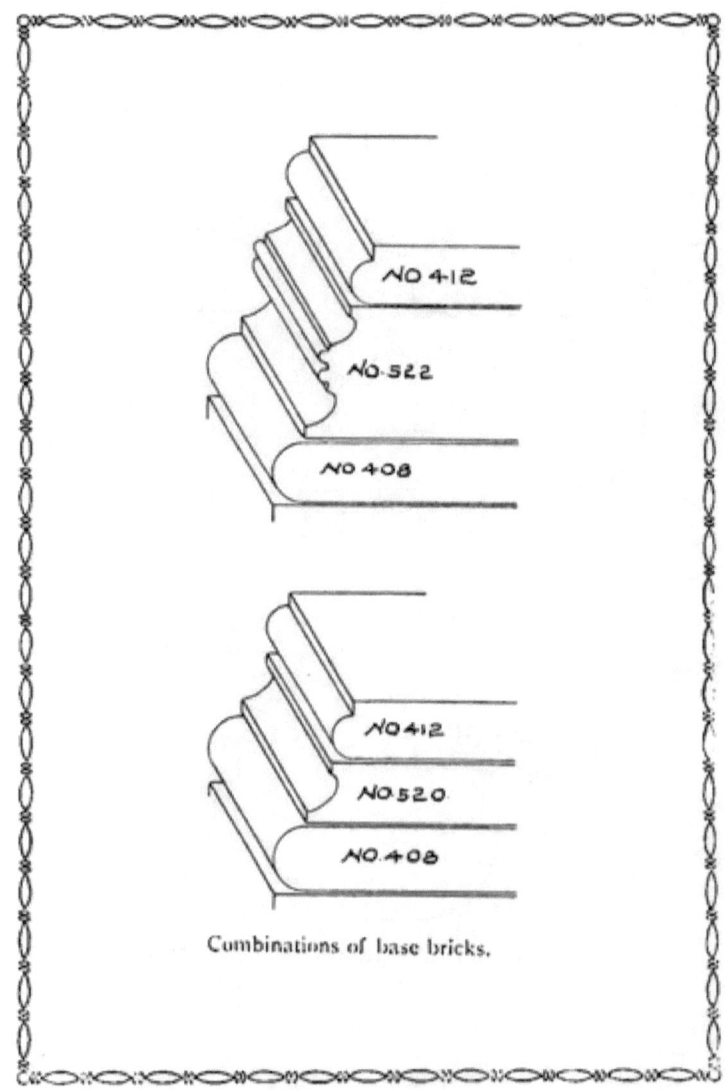

Combinations of base bricks.

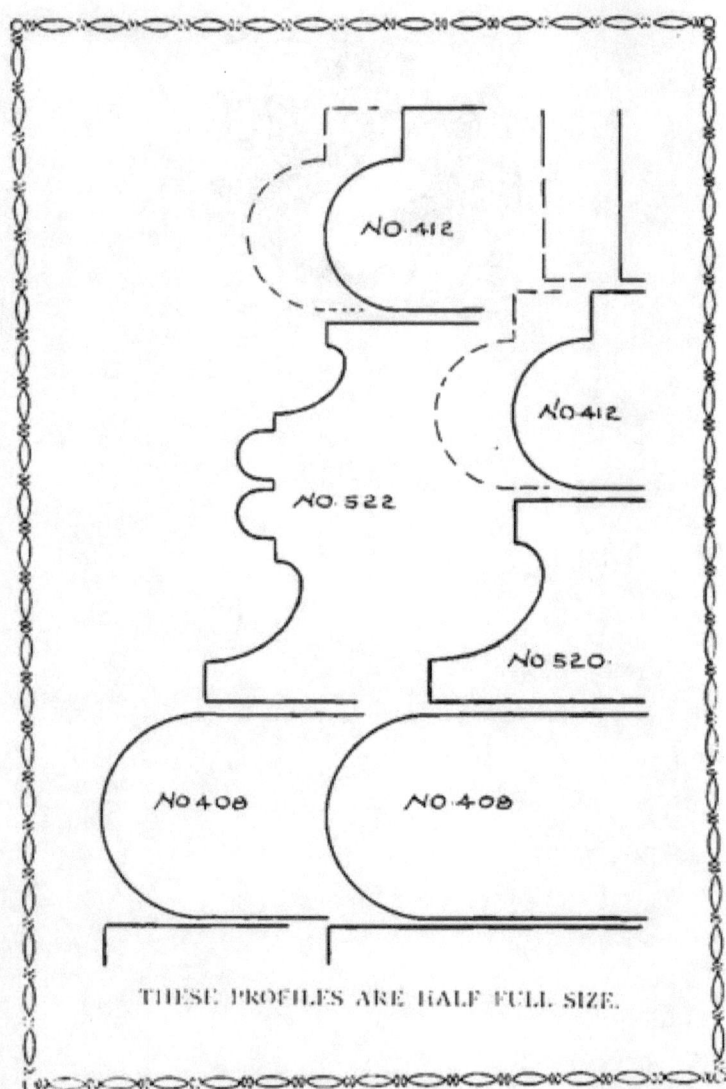

THESE PROFILES ARE HALF FULL SIZE.

SERIES K

ORNAMENTAL BRICKS

THE bricks of this series are useful for a variety of purposes. As they are here shown by drawings made from the bricks themselves, their actual appearance is readily understood.

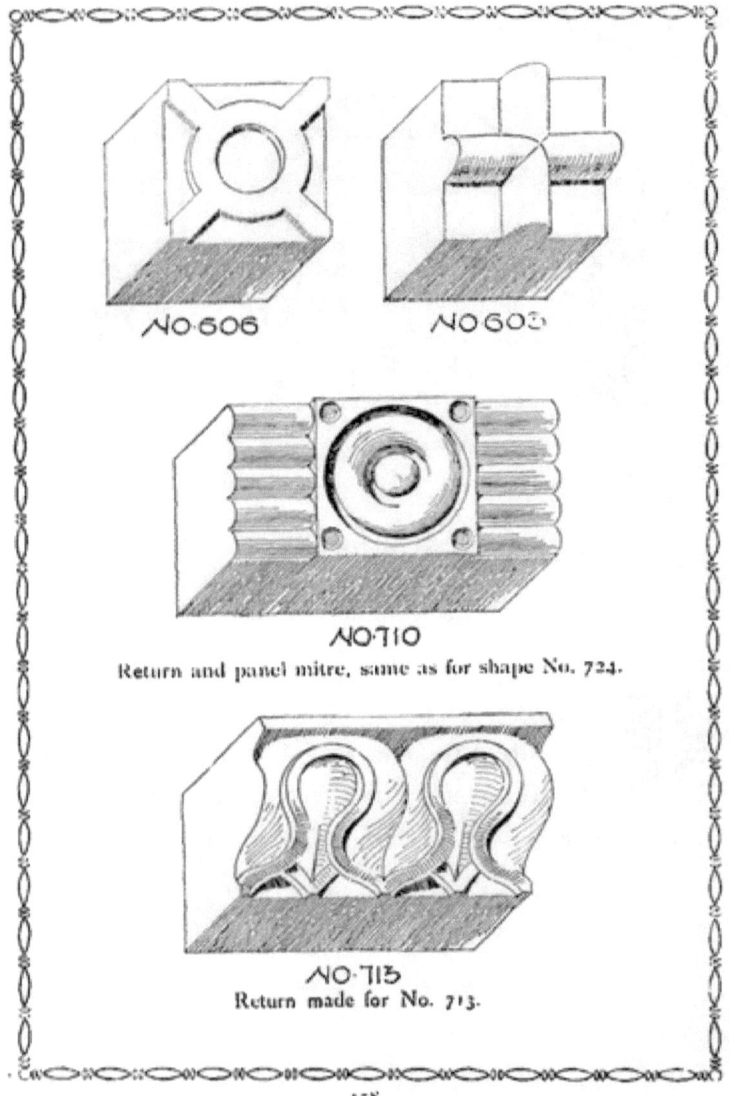

NO.606

NO.603

NO.710
Return and panel mitre, same as for shape No. 724.

NO.713
Return made for No. 713.

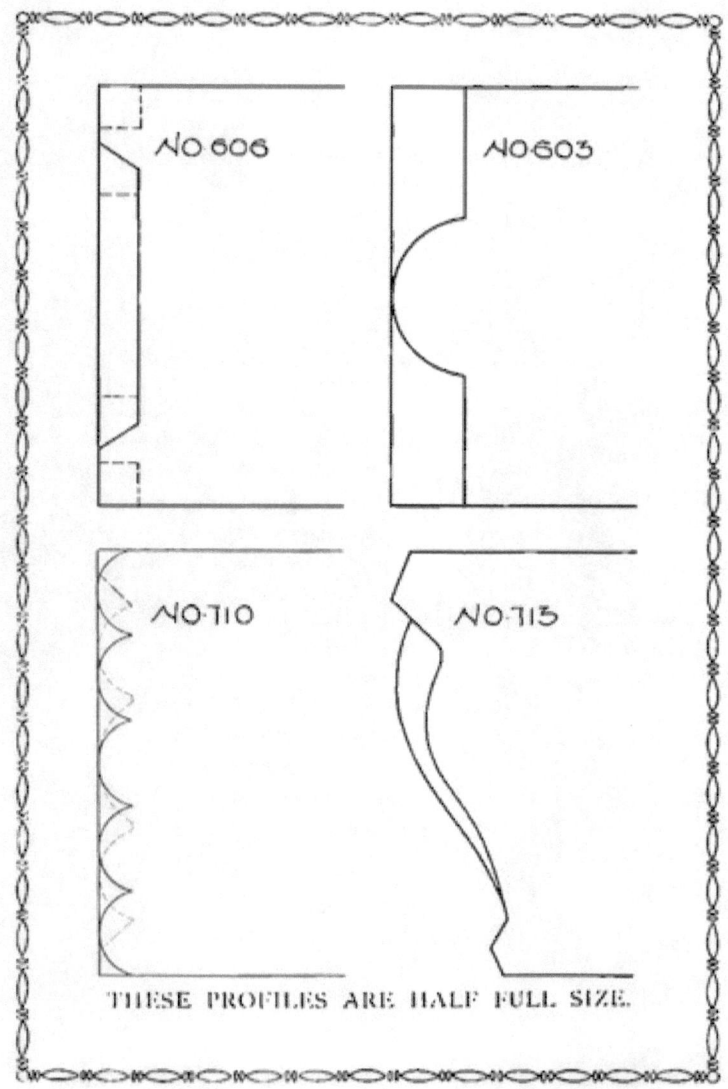

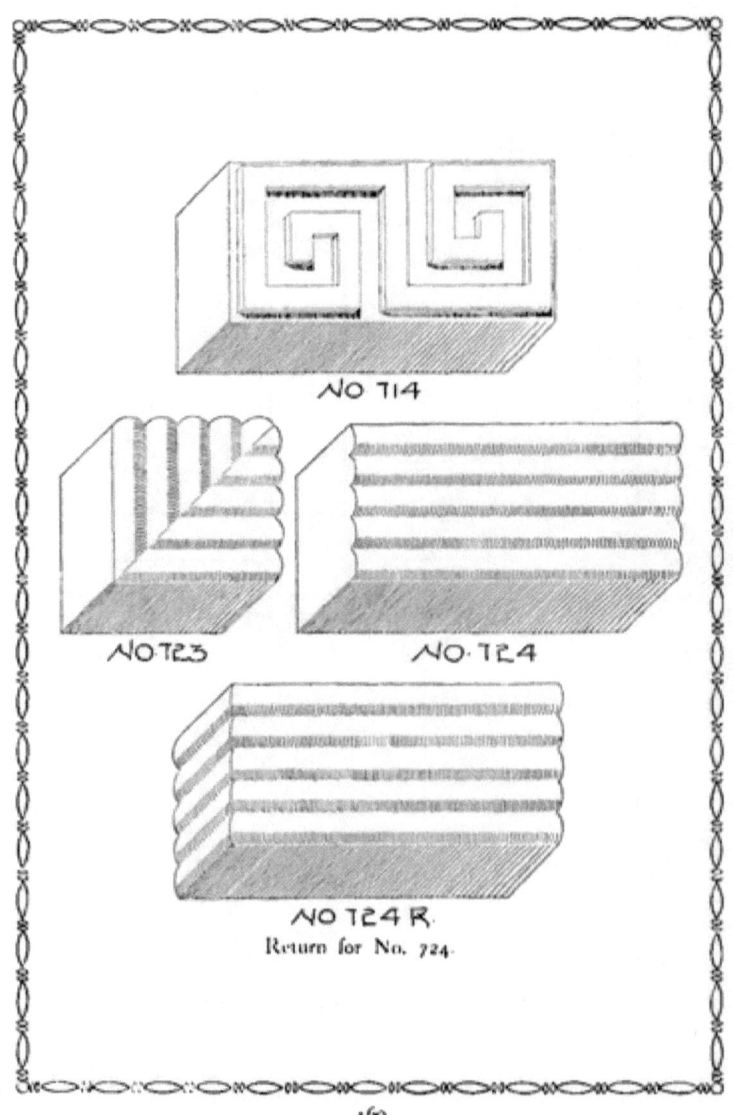

Return for No. 724.

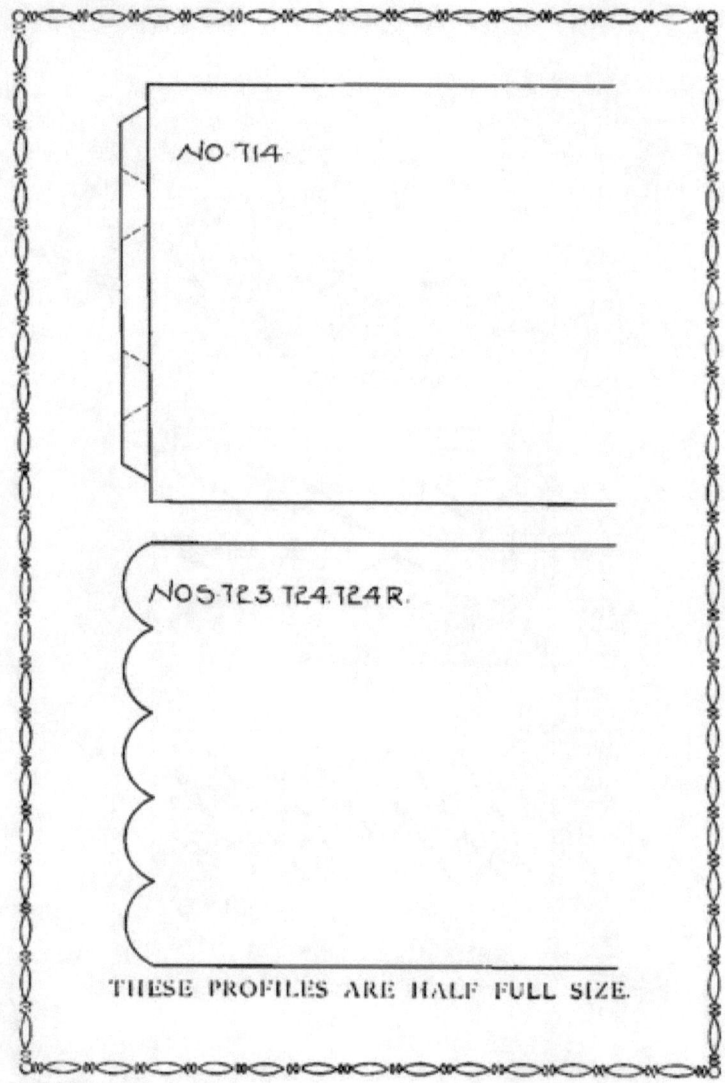

THESE PROFILES ARE HALF FULL SIZE.

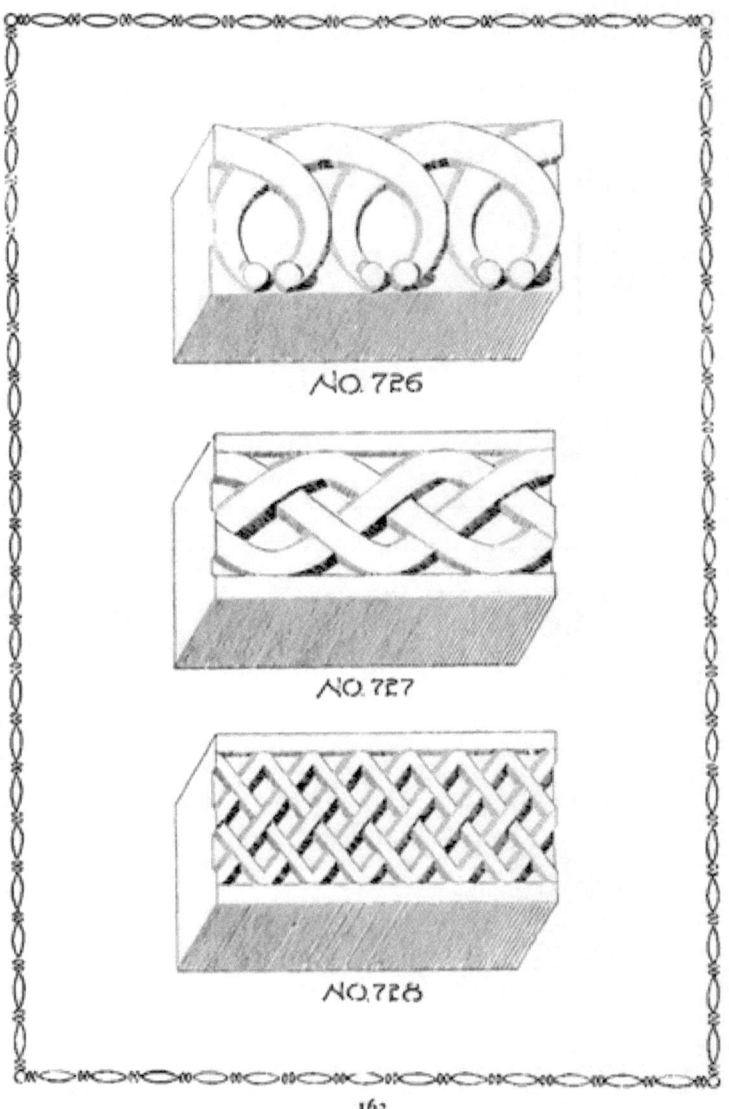

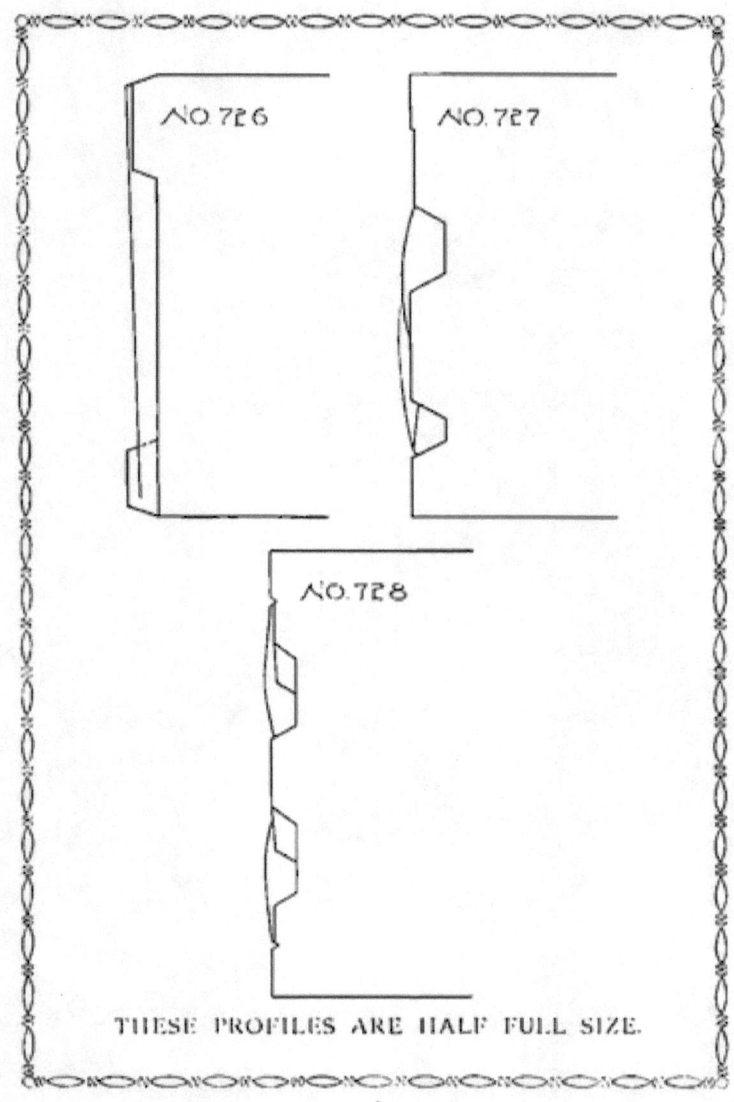

THESE PROFILES ARE HALF FULL SIZE.

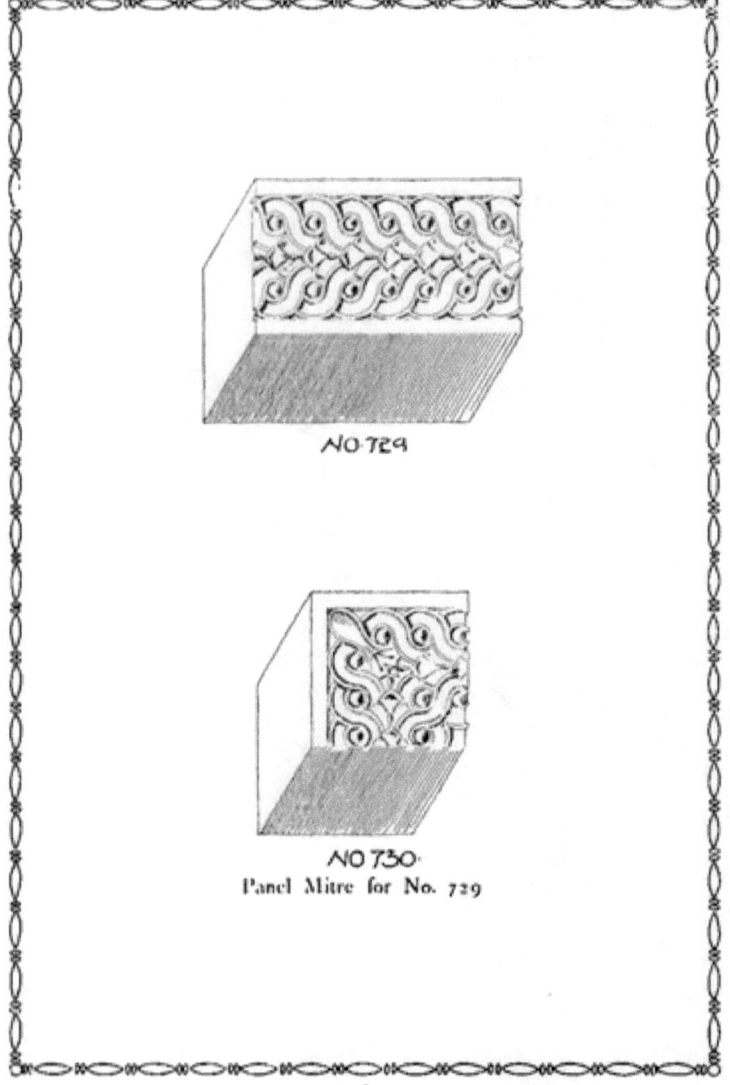

NO. 729

NO. 730.
Panel Mitre for No. 729

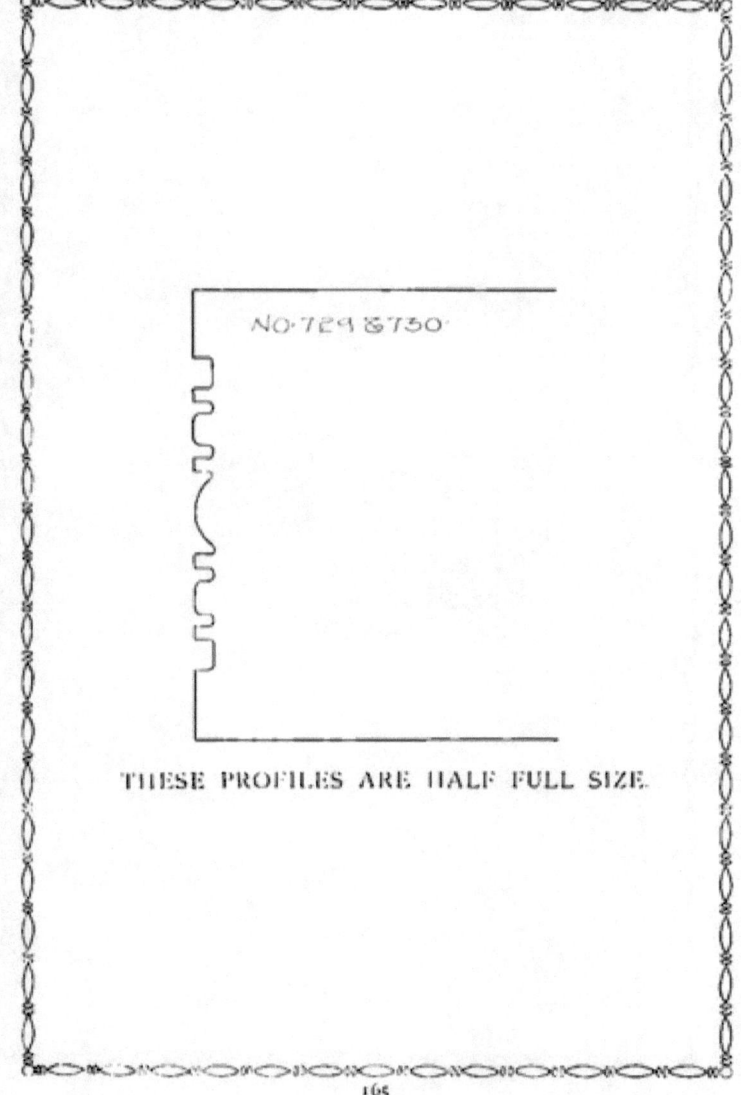

THESE PROFILES ARE HALF FULL SIZE.

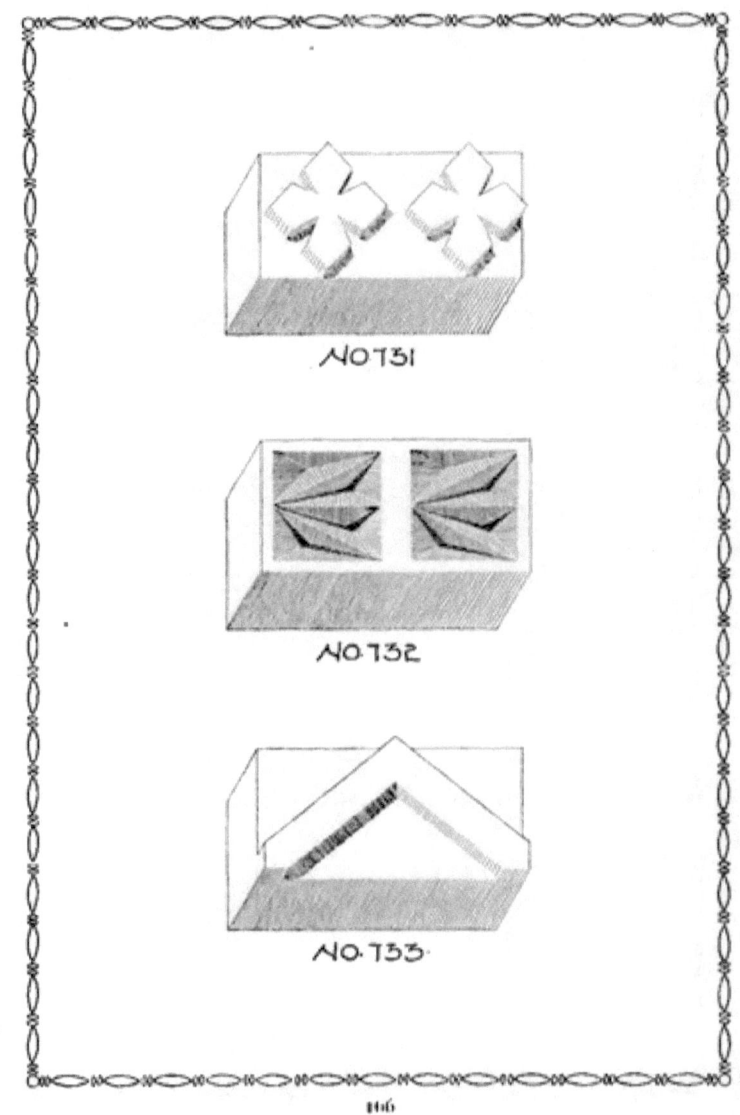

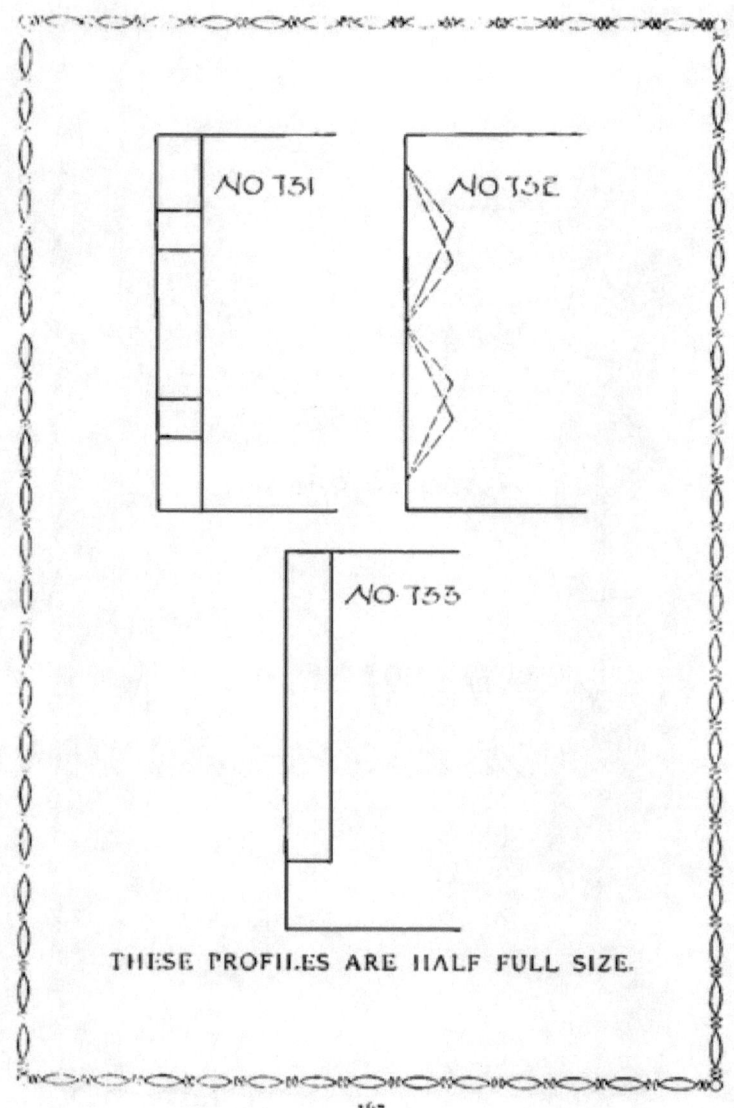

THESE PROFILES ARE HALF FULL SIZE.

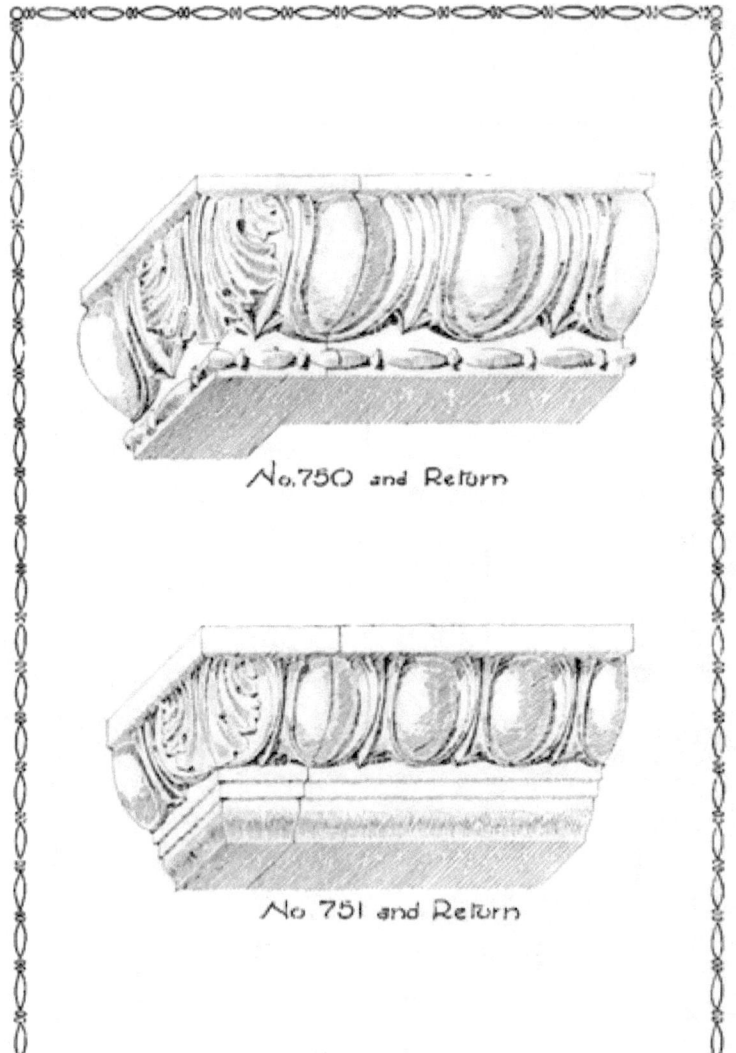

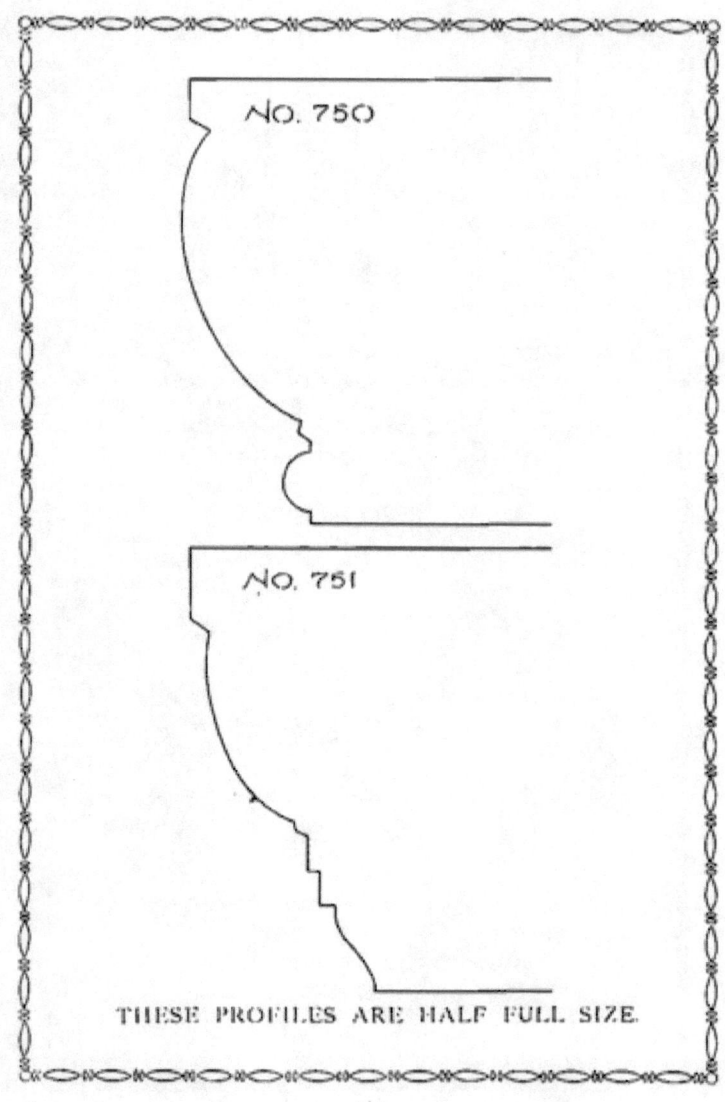

THESE PROFILES ARE HALF FULL SIZE.

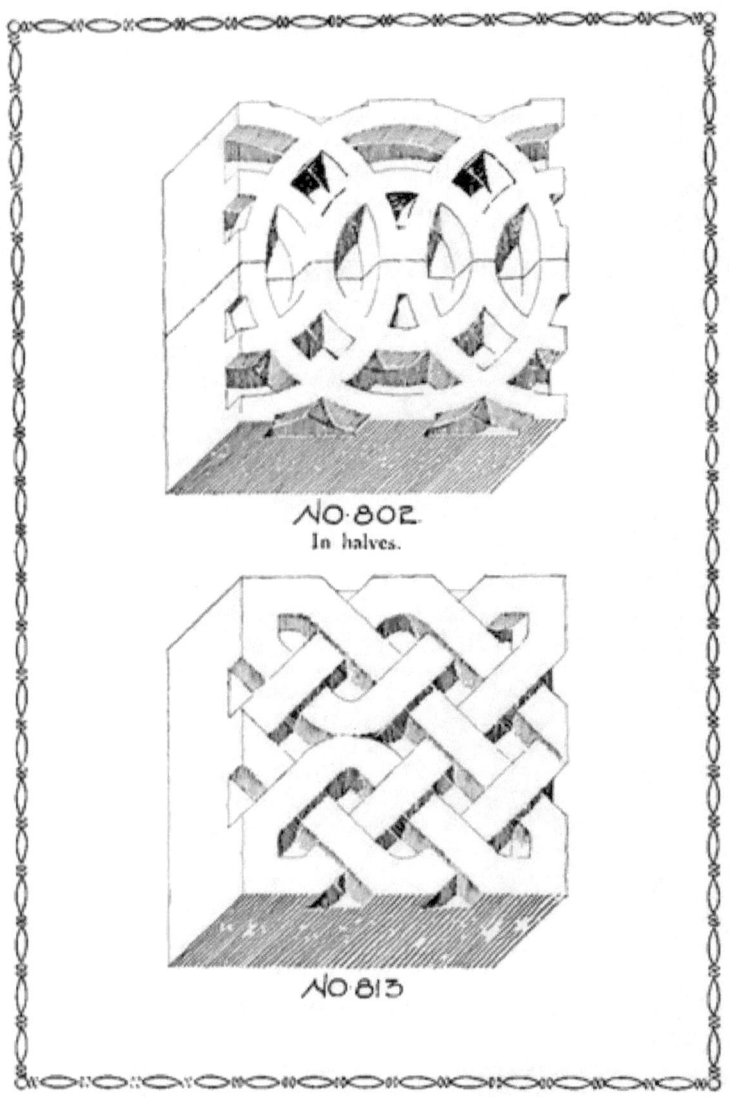

NO. 802.
In halves.

NO. 813

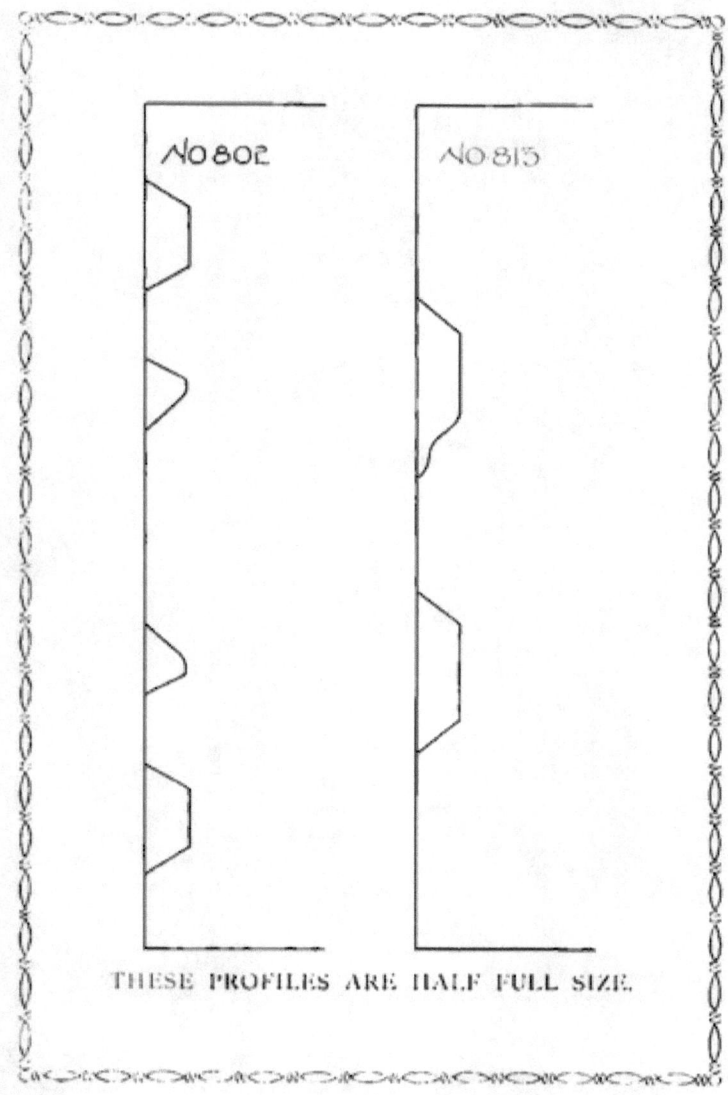

THESE PROFILES ARE HALF FULL SIZE.

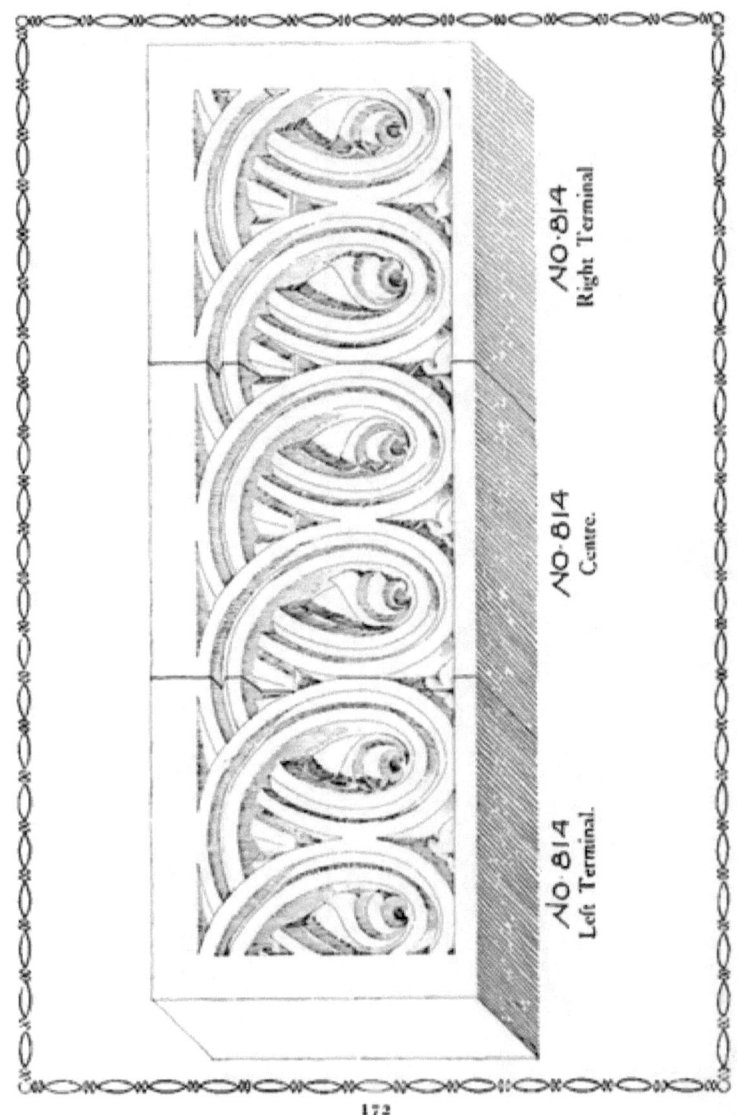

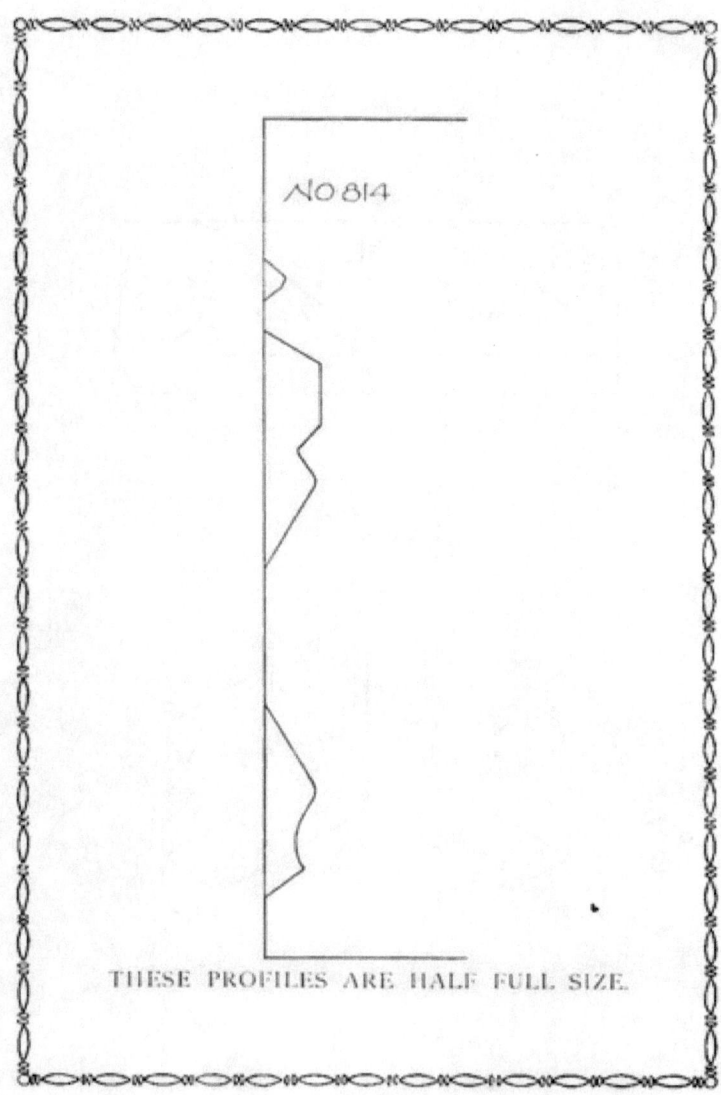

THESE PROFILES ARE HALF FULL SIZE.

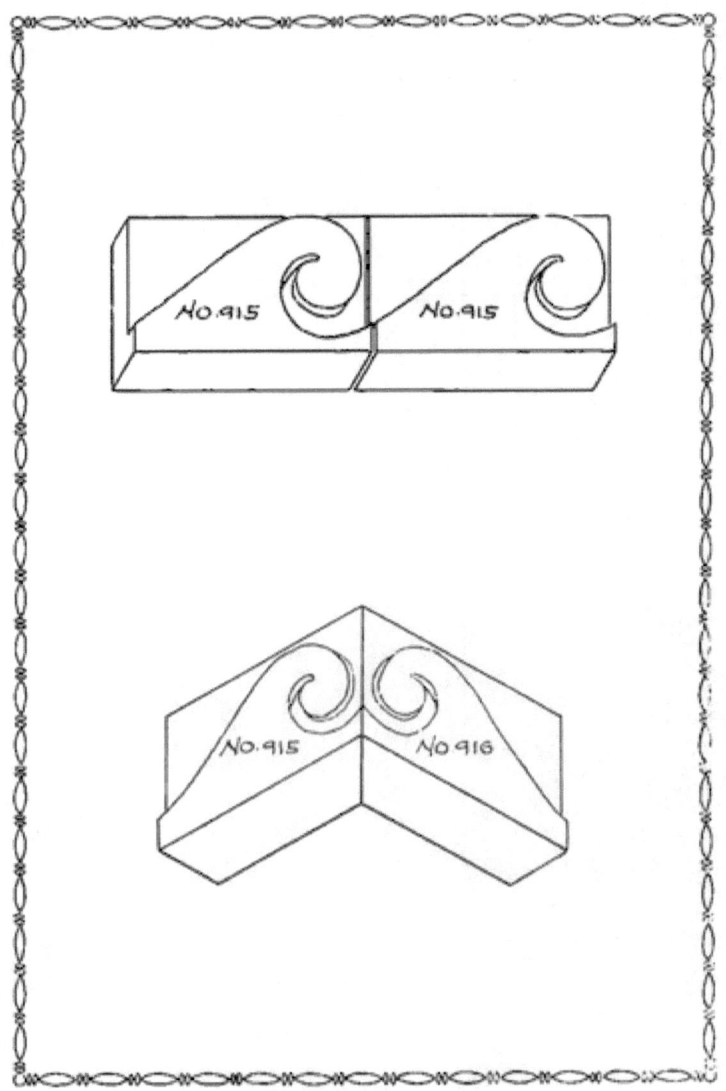

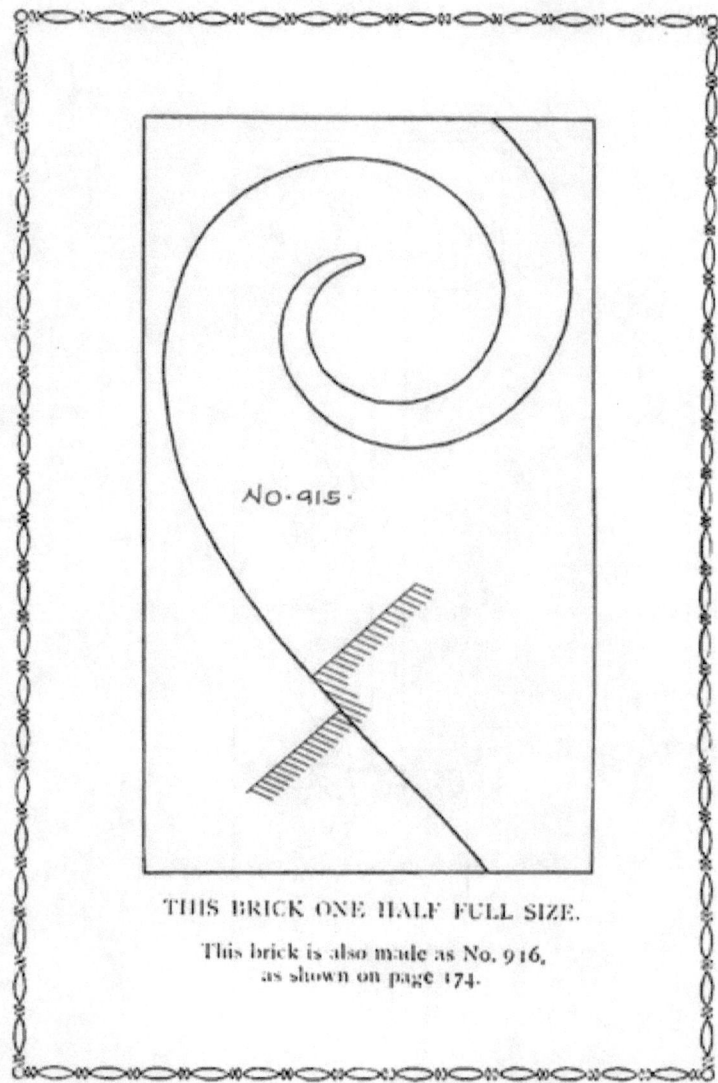

THIS BRICK ONE HALF FULL SIZE.

This brick is also made as No. 916, as shown on page 174.

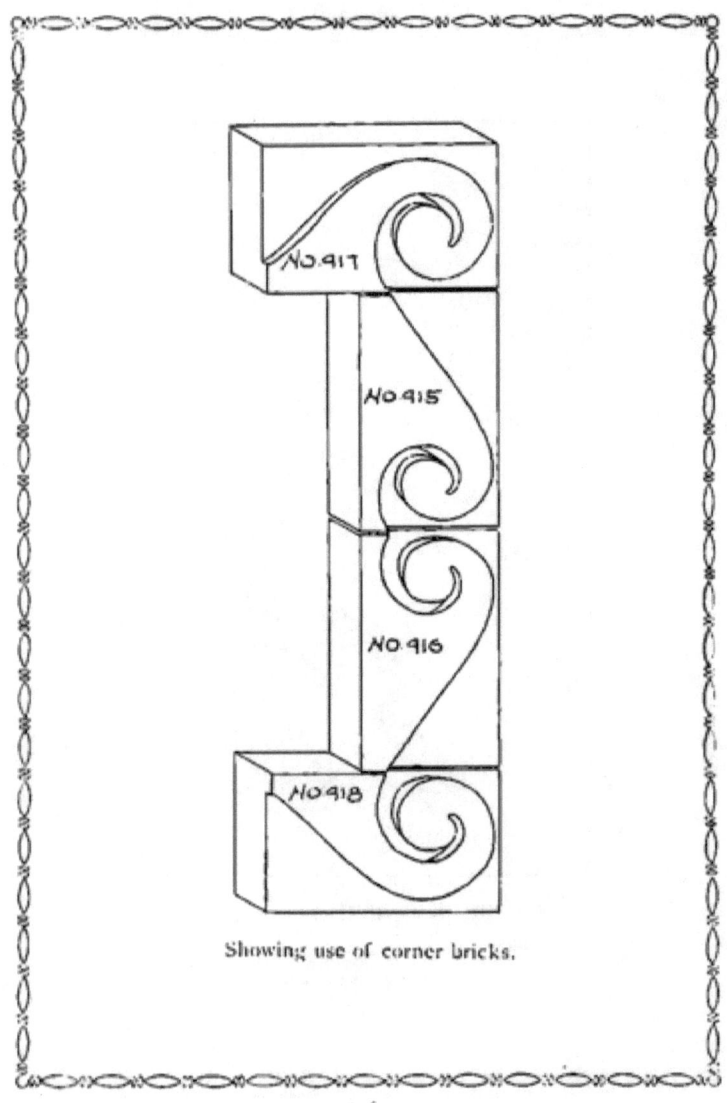

Showing use of corner bricks.

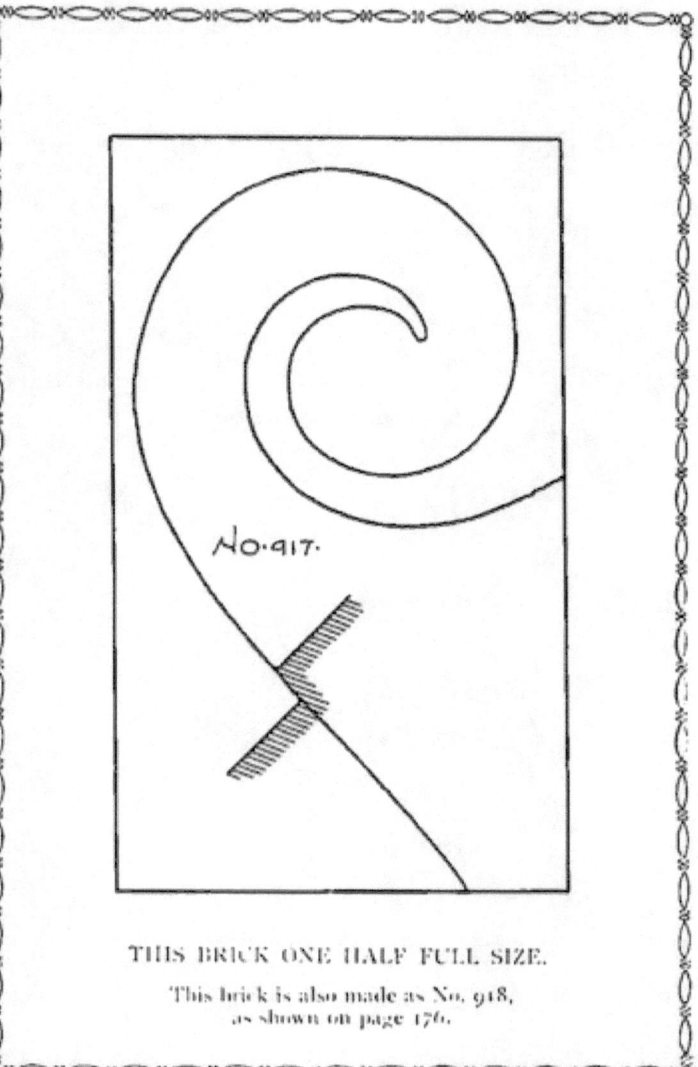

THIS BRICK ONE HALF FULL SIZE.

This brick is also made as No. 918,
as shown on page 176.

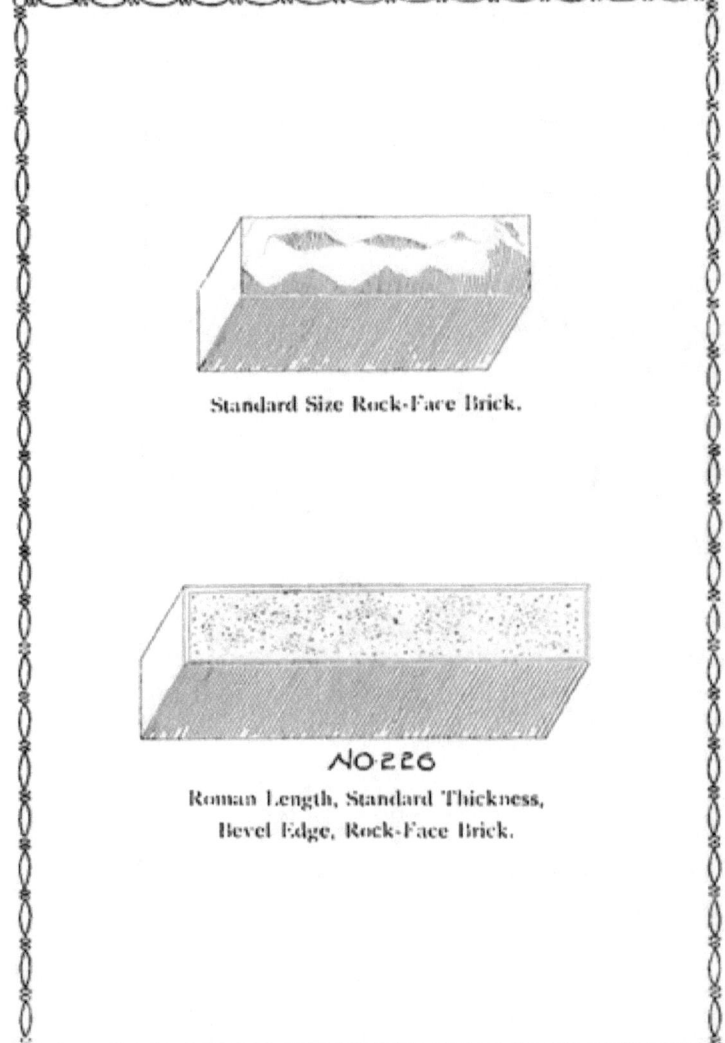

Standard Size Rock-Face Brick.

NO 226
Roman Length, Standard Thickness,
Bevel Edge, Rock-Face Brick.

INSTRUCTIONS FOR ORDERING

RICKS ordered by mistake or in excess of requirements will not be taken back.

Order moulded shapes eight weeks before you require them.

Furnish details for arches eight weeks before you require them.

Order as long as possible in advance of requirements,—better service can thus be obtained.

Mention date of catalogue from which shape numbers are specified.

Information as to sizes of bricks is given on page sixty-seven.

SEMI-CIRCULAR ARCHES

WE CAN MAKE THESE WITH MOULDED REVEALS

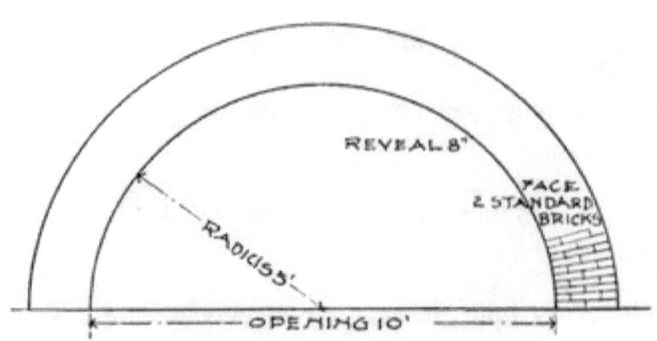

GIVE THE FOLLOWING DETAILS:

Width of opening.
Radius.
Depth of reveal or soffit.
Height of face.
If on piers, give width of pier.

Bricks can be ground for arches to be laid around segments, as in a tower or circular bay.

SEGMENT ARCHES

WE CAN MAKE THESE WITH MOULDED REVEALS

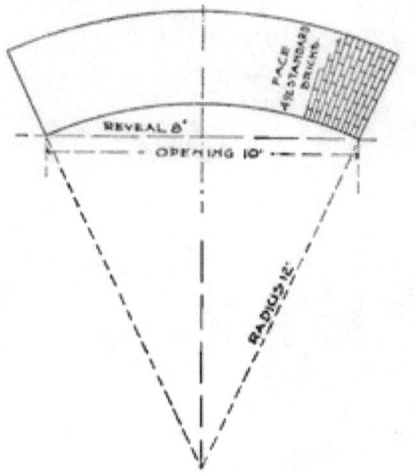

GIVE THE FOLLOWING DETAILS:

Width of opening.

Radius.

Depth of reveal or soffit.

Height of face.—Give inches, if laid with cut stone in skew-back. Give number of courses, if laid with bricks in skew-back.

If on piers, give width of pier.

Bricks can be ground for arches to be laid around segments, as in a tower or circular bay.

ELLIPTIC OR THREE-CENTRED ARCHES

WE CAN MAKE THESE WITH MOULDED REVEALS

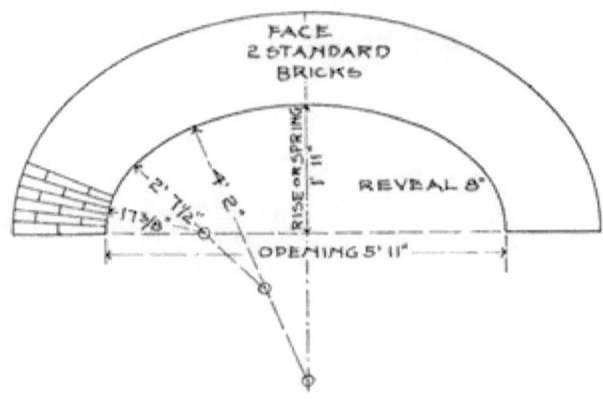

GIVE THE FOLLOWING DETAILS:

Width of opening.
Each of the three radii.
Rise or spring of arch.
Depth of reveal or soffit.
Height of face.
If on piers, give width of pier.

Bricks can be ground for arches to be laid around segments, as in a tower or circular bay.

GOTHIC ARCHES

WE CAN MAKE THESE WITH MOULDED REVEALS

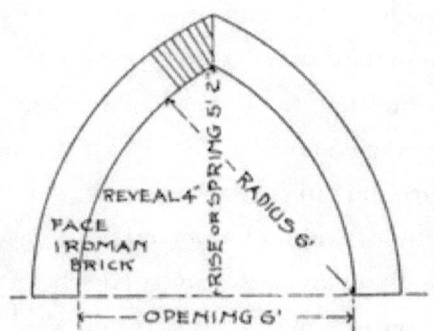

GIVE THE FOLLOWING DETAILS:

Width of opening.
Rise or spring of arch.
Radius.
Depth of reveal or soffit.
Height of face.
If on piers, give width of pier.

Unless otherwise specified, Gothic arches will be ground to one radius, as shown above.

Bricks can be ground for arches to be laid around segments, as in a tower or circular bay.

FLAT ARCHES

WE cannot make *flat* arches with moulded reveals. We can make moulded reveals in segment arches with flat top. When ground from gold, mottled, or Pompeiian bricks, the reveals of flat arches will show lighter color than face of arch.

When ground to skew-back for flat arch, with radius 1½ times width of opening:

> One Standard Stretcher gives height equal to three courses Standard size laid flat.
>
> One Roman Stretcher gives height equal to six courses Roman size laid flat.
>
> One Header, either Standard or Roman, gives height of three and an eighth to three and a quarter inches.

Multiples of any of the above give proportionate height. When radius is not as much as 1½ times the width of opening, it still further reduces the height obtained from each brick. When only four inches of reveal is required, we can make face of arch any height desired by grinding apparent headers from stretchers.

WE CANNOT MAKE FLAT ARCHES WITH MOULDED REVEALS

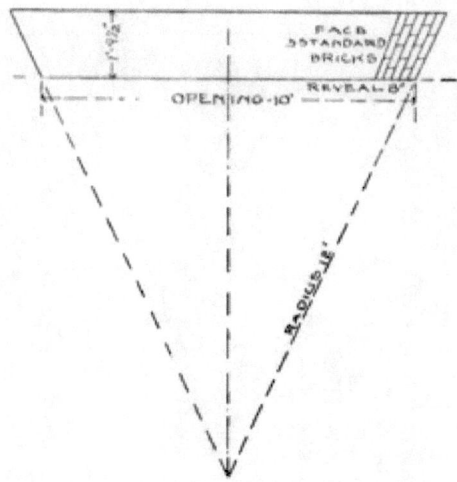

GIVE THE FOLLOWING DETAILS:

Width of opening.

Radius.

Depth of reveal.

Height of face.—Give inches, if laid with cut stone in skew-back. Give number of courses, if laid with bricks in skew-back.

If on piers, give width of pier.

Bricks can be ground for arches to be laid around segments, as in a tower or circular bay.

SEGMENT ARCHES WITH FLAT TOPS

WE CAN MAKE THESE WITH MOULDED REVEALS

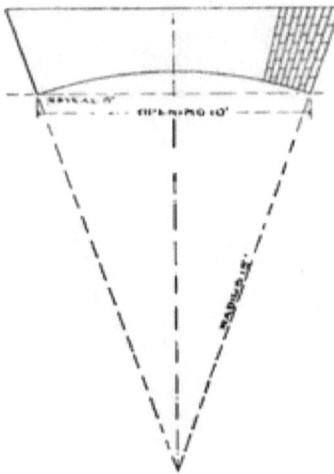

GIVE THE FOLLOWING DETAILS:

Width of opening.

Radius.

Depth of reveal.

Height of face.—Give inches, if laid with cut stone in skew-back. Give number of courses, if laid with bricks in skew-back.

If on piers, give width of pier.

Bricks can be ground for arches to be laid around segments, as in a tower or circular bay.

MITRES

State whether for return in string course around pilaster, or for panel mitre. Always specify whether *external* or *internal* angle. We show each of above in following cuts. Refer to *number* of cut when ordering.

No. 1.
External Angle.—String Course.

No. 2.
Internal Angle.—String Course.

No. 3.
External Panel Mitre.

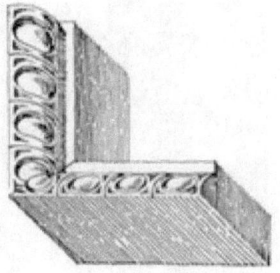

No. 4.
Internal Panel Mitre.

THE "HYDRAULIC-PRESS"

THE "Hydraulic-Press" Brick Co., of St. Louis, has, within the past twenty-seven years, so developed the art of brickmaking, that its productions have found favor in distant markets; and, to meet the wide-spread and growing demand for bricks of its manufacture, has, from time to time, erected new works in various localities, as shown on the opposite page.

Bricks made by the "Hydraulic-Press" Brick Co., and its various branches, may be seen in the finest brick buildings of the principal cities in the United States.

The Companies manufacture over three hundred million bricks per annum.

THE COMPANIES' OFFICES

HE offices of the various Companies are located as below. Address the nearest Company for samples and prices.

Hydraulic-Press Brick Co.	St. Louis, Mo.
Eastern Hydraulic-Press Brick Co.	Philadelphia, Pa.
New York " " " "	Rochester, N. Y.
Washington	Washington, D. C.
Chicago	Chicago, Ill.
Kansas City "	Kansas City, Mo.
Findlay	Findlay, Ohio.
Omaha	Omaha, Neb.
Illinois	St. Louis, Mo.
Northern	Minneapolis, Minn.
Akron "	Cleveland, Ohio.

Salesroom for New York and New England is located Room 4, ninth story, Metropolitan Building, Twenty-third and Madison Avenue, New York City.

www.ingramcontent.com/pod-product-compliance
Lightning Source LLC
Chambersburg PA
CBHW020912230426
43666CB00008B/1431